Return to the Planet of the Apes

Jorge Consuegra

DEEP SPACE.
No atmosphere, no life, nothing. Just a web of lights- a billion stars hang in a velvet void. The only sound is the howl of the cosmic wind.
The light of a distant sun strikes a rising planet. We see ragged continents and oceans wreathed in cloud. This is earth rise. Our world spins slowly in space, a thing of beauty, of awesome majesty. In all this nothingness - life.
We push in on the planet - in to the Americas. The wind grows louder -

A PUEBLO VILLAGE.
A broken-down pick-up bumps into a God-forsaken villagea cluster of adobe houses, blinding flurries of dust and sand. The pick-up stops in front of a crumbling church. A man in his 60s gets out carrying a medical bag. This is the DOCTOR. '

A WOMAN'S FACE.
Screaming. She's very young - a South American Indian - lying on a bed in a corner of one of the houses. She is in the final throes of childbirth, a sheet draped over her loins. The Doctor works between her legs, encouraging her in Spanish.
The local PRIEST, not long out of the seminary, crouches at her side counting off the beads of a rosary. He looks like he is about to pass out.

SUDDENLY THE WOMAN BITES DOWN HARD ON HER LIP. A THIN LINE OF BLOOD COURSES
DOWN HER CHIN. THE BREATH EXPLODES FROM HER LUNGS AS SHE PUSHES REALLY HARD
DOCTOR
Arriva!
He lifts the child from her loins, but it makes no sound. We don't see the baby - just the shock on the Doctor's face. The mother struggles up to see her child.
The Doctor grabs the sheet from her torso and covers the baby with it. He thrusts the bundle into the Priest's hands.

DOCTOR (CONT'D)
(in Spanish)
Dead - the child is dead. Now go!
We hold on the mother's anguished face. Dissolve to

A HELICOPTER
Off the roof of a tall hospital building. As it rises up into the night we see a red cross painted on its side. It's an air ambulance.
The chopper turns away. The Manhattan skyline, every skyscraper a blaze of lights, opens up behind it. The chopper swoops over the Brooklyn bridge and into the night.

GROVE OF TREES
Winter's coming on - every leaf is a different shade of amber and gold. The helicopter drops down between the branches and lands on an immaculately tended lawn. Surrounding it are the gracious buildings of a great university. Harvard.

Two paramedics clamber out of the back of the helicopter and load a stainless steel casket onto a gurney. They wheel it fast towards one of the buildings. As they go' through the front doors, we hold on a sign etched into the stone

DEPARTMENT OF BIOLOGY
A PAIR OF MECHANICAL HANDS
slide a long cylindrical "key" into the stainless steel casket. We pull back to reveal the casket lies in a sealed, uncontaminated room. A group of people in lab coats -scientists and researchers - stare through the glass walls.
A young TECHNICIAN, working at a console, keyboards in a series of commands.
Sswhish. The top of the steel casket swings open. Clouds of white gas stream out - whatever's inside has been nitrogen cooled.
The gas clears. Lying inside is the body of a newborn child - except that the baby has the skin, the face and the features of a man of eighty. The scientists and the researchers react - shocked.
One of the mechanical hands glides towards the baby. In its fingers it holds a long steel scalpel. This is the highest-tech autopsy you've ever seen. The scalpel drives down, about to open the chest cavity -

BLOOD SPRAYS
But not from the baby's chest - it's in glass vials, exploding as white-hot flames consume them. A plastic-gloved lab assistant, silhouetted against the flames, is emptying hospital waste into a furnace. He slams the door shut.
He turns we see his face. He's in his 4Os, handsome in a rough-hewn way - a strong jaw and a muscular body. There's a cool intelligence in his eyes, but a two-day beard and a worn-out uniform make him look like a man who, between youth and middle-age, lost his way. And so he has. His name is WILL

ROBINSON.
He takes a steel trolley, wheels it through a set of swing doors and out of sight.

CLOSED CIRCUIT TV SCREEN
features the image of one of the scientists we recognize from the autopsy.
She's in her 30s - attractive, long hair left loose on her shoulders, an air of authority about her. Her name is BILLIE RAE DIAMOND. She is a Professor of Biology.
We tilt down from the screen. It hangs from a wall in a deserted laboratory
-overhead lights, rows and rows of wire animal cages. Moving down death row, feeding the lab animals, is Will Robinson.

TWO SAD-EYED CHIMPS, CLEANING EACH OTHER IN THEIR TINY CAGE, TURN AND STARE
AT HIM. SUDDENLY WILL STOPS - HE'S HEARD SOMETHING ON THE SCREEN THAT HAS
CAUGHT HIS ATTENTION. HE TURNS AND LOOKS -
DIAMOND

The exact cause of death is still unknown. What is certain - we're dealing with something we've never seen before. Every organ in the body is affected...
Superimposed over Diamond's face is a three dimensional, computer-generated graphic of the baby's body.
Will forgets about what he's doing. He walks towards the screen. We push in on it.
Screeds of new data appear
Vascular System ....Atrophied
Neurological Function ....Senile dementia
We hold on Will's eyes - he stares at it.

AN AUDITORIUM
Billy Rae Diamond stands on a podium continuing her briefing. About forty scientists are sitting in front of her in a dimly-lit lecture hall.
Diamond is even more impressive in person - she is tall and gracious but you don't become a Professor at Harvard' at her age without having an iron will and a sparkling intelligence. She speaks with great authority -

DIAMOND (CONT'D)
The baby in question, Michael James Flanagan -she points at the computer-generated graphic on a huge screen was born at New York Hospital yesterday.

MAP OF THE WORLD ILLUMINATES AN ADJOINING SCREEN -
DIAMOND
But the Center for Disease Control in Atlanta has received similar reports from a village in Bolivia, two cities in Australia, seven countries in
Europe, a cluster of cases in Namibia and Mexico. Forty-two cases in all.
As she speaks, pinpoints of light on the map identify the exact locations.
They dot their way across the entire globe. Dr Diamond turns to face her audience-

DIAMOND (CONT'D)
Like Michael Flanagan, they were full-term babies. Two hundred and seventy eight days since conception and yet, by all reasonable medical standards, they have completed their entire life cycle. They have gone from conception to death, not in three score years and ten, but in slightly less than nine months. Michael Flanagan died of old age.
Silence as Diamond lets the scientists and researchers absorb it. On a balcony high above, another man is taking notes. He sits alone, almost hidden in shadow. It's Will Robinson.

SHEETS OF ICE ON A SHUTTER DOOR
Will crouches in front of a row of self-storage units on the edge of town.
It's night, the place is deserted. He slips a rusted key into a padlock.
Snapl The key breaks.
Will curses. He grabs a piece of timber and pulls a nail out of it. He slides the nail into the padlock and manipulates the tumblers. The padlock springs open.

SPIDERS weave a web in a corner of the storage unit. A work light hangs from the ceiling. Will is ripping open stacks of boxes from long ago. He puts together a pile of yellowing files and old floppy disks.

**PULLS OUT A CASSETTE TAPE AND STARES AT IT, UNSURE WHAT'S ON IT. HE TAKES A
CASSETTE PLAYER FROM OUT OF THE JUNK, SLIDES IT IN AND PRESSES "PLAY"A HUGE
ROUND OF APPLAUSE. AS IT DIES, WE HEAR A MAN'S VOICE. IT'S WILL, SPEAKING
FROM YEARS AGO -
WILL**
(on tape)
I would like to thank the faculty and staff for this great honor...
We push in on Will's face as he listens to himself...

WILL (CONT'D) have had the opportunity to work with three talented colleagues. I'm privileged to also call them my friends -
A shadow of pain crosses his face. He shuts off the tape and sits motionless.

LAFAYETTE PARK
Night. Homeless people in the park build cardboard shelters against a coming storm. Across the road, the first drops of rain splatter against the
White House.
A string of Government cars pass through the huge gates and pull up in front of the West Portico. From inside, we hear a man's voice - well-spoken, authoritative

PRESIDENT (O.S.)
There's no mistake - you're sure?

JEFFERSON LIBRARY
Diamond sits in the President's study - book-lined walls, a fire in the hearth. A group of men sit on the sofasthe Surgeon-General, the Chief of
Staff, the National Security Advisor, the Secretaw of Health. A table is littered with graphs end files.

DIAMOND
We've got five thousand cases now, Mr President. That's in three weeks. The number is doubling every hundred and sixty-eight hours.
The President stands near a window, half in shadow, the firelight playing across his face. He's in his 50's but the strain of office makes him look older.

DIAMOND (CONT'D)
That's a geometric progression, sir. In three months there'll be over seven million cases. After that we hit the wall -
She pushes a thick, bound volume across the table.

DIAMOND (CONT'D)
According to this, there won't be a live birth on the planet.
The President looks at her for a moment. Then he reaches down and picks up the bound volume. It's hundreds of pages of numbers and projections.

PRESIDENT
These are just computer projections - species don't disappear that fast.

DIAMOND
Tell that to the dinosaurs, sir.
He looks out the window at the winter storm sweeping down on them.

NATIONAL SECURITY ADVISOR
What date - when exactly do we hit this wall?

DIAMOND
Six months and twenty-one days.
Silence. The President keeps looking out the window.

PRESIDENT
Can't somebody tell me - what exactly are we dealing with. Is it a virus or what?

DIAMOND
We don't know, sir.
The President turns to the Chief of Staff.

PRESIDENT
Whatever they need, Bob - anything. Harry Truman put together the Manhattan Project - you understand?
The Chief of Staff nods his head - yes.

PRESIDENT (CONT'D)
(softly)
A world without children - it's inconceivable. And what about the rest of us
- what do we do? Just sit and watch our species die? Will the last person to leave the planet turn out the lights.
Silence again. Finally a young woman - the White House Press Secretary - speaks.

PRESS SECRETARY
We're going to have to manage the public. Right now, the truth may be inoperative -

PRESIDENT
Of course we're going to have to manage itl We're going to have to manage a whole lot of things. But can't we take at least one moment to be human?
He looks around the room. We hold on their somber faces.

A CHEAP APARTMENT
Through the window - the neon sign of a gas station. This is Will's place,
He lives alone - a bed in the corner, run-down furniture, dishes in the sink.
The kitchen table has been turned into a desk - Will sits at an old computer, surrounded
by the yellowing stacks of files and floppy disks. He stares at the screen - the notes and
equations are blurred. He's been at this so long, he can barely focus. He rubs his hand
across his eyes.
A small mewing sound. Will turns to an alcove in the corner - a cat lies in a basket,
panting. Will goes to her.
She's giving birth - the first of her new-born kittens lies next to her.
Will strokes the mother's head, looking at the miracle of new life. He puts his fingers in
a water bowl, about to moisten the mother's mouth.
Then he stops. He looks again at the kitten - there's two of them now. A beat as he just
stares -

WILL
(softly)
Jesus Christ... of course!

A LUXURIOUS BATHROOM
Through frosted glass we see the silhouette of a woman taking a shower.
Whoever she is, she's got a great figure. The sound of a doorbell. The shower door opens
-Diamond sticks her head out. She looks at a clock - it's almost midnight.

VIDEO ENTRY PHONE
A video screen monitors the front door. On it we see Will - his hair tousled, an old
overcoat buttoned to the neck, a battered briefcase under his arm.
Diamond - a towel around her shoulders, hair dripping - picks up the phone.

DIAMOND
Who is it?

WILL (O.S.)
Will Robinson.

DIAMOND
I think you have the wrong house.

WILL (O.S.)
I work at the department.
He turns and looks straight into the camera. Instinctively, Diamond covers her breasts.
She looks at him - recognition dawns.

AN ELEGANT ROOM

Will and Diamond sit in the living room of a gracious townhouse - wooden floors and beautiful rugs. Diamond doesn't wear any make-up -just jeans and an oversized shirt. She looks even more beautiful. It does nothing to ease
Will's nerves. He's got his briefcase open in front of him, speaking from sheaves of notes and papers.

DIAMOND
(interrupting)
Hold on - how do you know about the case load? The Government's trying to manage this - they've withheld that information.

WILL
The Internet, Doctor. It's a highway - you can ride it anywhere you want. I got into 'the Center for Disease Control. I had a look at their raw data.

DIAMOND
Jesus. Do you know what you're doing? This is the White House we're talking about.

WILL
(Heated))
No, it's a disease and it doesn't come any worse than this - that's what we're talking about.

HE LOOKS AWAY, CALMING HIMSELF. HE SHUFFLES HIS NOTES. HE SPEAKS AGAIN,
QUIETLY -
WILL
I've listened at the lab - I think I know where you're looking. Bacterias mostly, but there's a strong push into the retro-viruses. You're wrong,
Doctor.

DIAMOND
Really - and I thought I was arrogant. But then, I'm just a professor.

WILL
No virus or bacteria has ever discriminated on the grounds of sex.

DIAMOND
I can think of one.

WILL
Sure, it can start in pockets but it never stays there. This thing does. It only affects women of child-bearing age. What - it's so smart it can recognize motherhood? I don't think so. No, this is into the very heart of what we are. This is genetic. This is part of the DNA.

DIAMOND
Thank you. A hundred thousand genes make up human DNA - that really narrows it down.

WILL
As a matter of fact it does. There's only one part of the DNA that's passed exclusively through women. Thirty-seven genes, the oldest part of the human organism -

DIAMOND
(realizing)
The mitochondrial DNA.

WILL
Over the years there's been speculation -not all of it crazy either - that somehow it triggers aging, He slides a sheaf of yellowing extracts from scientific journals across the table. She doesn't pay them any attention - she's thinking.

DIAMOND
You realize what you're saying, don't you? A bacteria - I think we'd get it for sure. A virus -you'd have to say we've got a chance. But say you're right. The mitochondrial DNA - that's so far out on the frontier, we can barely see it.

WILL
Like I said - it doesn't get any worse than this.
She keeps staring down at the documents and notes lying on the table. A beat.

WILL (CONT'D)
Are you okay?

DIAMOND
Sure.

WILL LOOKS AT HER FOR A MOMENT -
WILL
Shit. You're pregnant, aren't you?

DIAMOND
Nine weeks.

THEIR EYES MEET - SHE SHRUGS, TRYING TO PUT A BRAVE FACE ON IT. SHE GETS TO
HER FEET -
DIAMOND
Do you want a drink - coffee, a sandwich or something?

WILL

(Recoiling)
No...no, I'm fine thanks.
Watches as he picks up his papers and puts them back in his battered briefcase.

AN EMPTY STREET
It's late at night. Will clutches his briefcase under his arm, heading home. A bitter wind blows out of the north. He looks a lonely and forlorn figure as he makes his way through the pools of light cast by the streetlights.

CONVOY OF N.A.S.A. TRUCKS
RUMBLE THROUGH THE EARLY MORNING - THE CITY IS JUST WAKING. THE TRUCKS,
DOZENS OF WHITE EIGHTEEN-WHEELERS, TURN THROUGH THE FRONT GATES OF HARVARD.
THEY STOP IN FRONT OF THE GROVE OF TREES. WE CRANE UP FROM THEM TO A WINDOW
IN THE BIOLOGY BUILDING -
HAND HITS A TABLE
IT'S DIAMOND - SHE'S ANGRY. BREAKFAST TRAYS CLUTTER THE TABLE -SHE'S IN THE
MIDDLE OF A CONFERENCE WITH A GROUP OF SCIENTISTS. SHE GLARES AT AN
ARROGANT YOUNG NEUROLOGIST -
DIAMOND
It's just an idea, Bob. All we're doing is taking it for a walk around the block.
A man in his 60s - distinguished, diplomatic - intercedes.

DE MAUPASSANT
There was a lot of work done on it in the 7Os. I can't recall the details but someone had the idea that mitochondriel DNA was like a genetic memory.
If you could unlock it, you could physically travel back down it. Through evolution - like a time machine.

BOB
Wowl Those 70s, man. I'm really sorry I missed them.
Everyone - Diamond included - laughs.

OLD PHOTOS OF A SAILING BOAT
They hang on the wall of a tiny room - not an office, just a hole-in-the-wall Will has turned into his own. He sits at a table, making notes. A knock - Diamond enters.

DIAMOND
I thought you'd like to know - we're looking at mitochondrial DNA,

WILL
Thanks for telling me.

THEY LOOK AT ONE ANOTHER. IT'S AN AWKWARD MOMENT - NEITHER ONE QUITE SURE WHETHER OR HOW TO CONTINUE THE CONVERSATION. DIAMOND SEES THE PHOTOS -

DIAMOND
Is that you?
She points at a man in his 20s standing on the deck in one of the photos, Will nods.

DIAMOND (CONT'D)
Seattle. Is that where you went to school?
Will hesitates - we sense that he doesn't really want to answer.

WILL
No. Princeton.

DIAMOND
Expensive.

WILL
A scholarship. Then I did some post-graduate work... I never really finished.
Something in the way Will says it - some sense of loss - makes Diamond pause. She recovers and looks in her wallet. She pulls out a photograph and hands it to Will. It shows a small sailing boatgaff-rigged and a varnished hull.

WILL (CONT'D)
It's a Kestrel 24 - I haven't seen one of those in years. She's a beautiful boati

DIAMOND
My grandfather left it to me. I don't sail it much any more - it's too hard to find a for'etd hand.

WILL
What about your husband - doesn't he sail.

DIAMOND
I don't know - I haven't met him yet.

WILL LOOKS AT HER. HIS EXPRESSION SAYS IT - WHAT? SHE SHRUGS -

DIAMOND
I wanted a baby but I'm thirty-four-years old. Sooner or later you realize that somewhere along the way you've missed the man you've been waiting for.

WILL

What did you do - ask a friend?

DIAMOND
I thought of it.

WILL
Lucky friend.

DIAMOND
I went to a clinic. Not exactly romantic, but it worked.
(pauses)
Good idea, bad timing.

WILL
How many people have you put on the mDNA?

DIAMOND
Seven.

WILL
That's all?!

DIAMOND
That's all I can spare. It's just a theory -one of dozens of theories.
Will looks away in disgust.

DIAMOND (CONT'D)
What is it with you - it's not just science is it? Why are you so passionate about this?

WILL
I know I'm right. It's a mutation. A hundred thousand years it's probably been lying there -shifting, weaving into the mDNA. You either go back and change evolution or you engineer it out. Seven peopleYou might as well shoot peas at a dam.

DIAMOND
You haven't answered my question - why so passionate?

WILL
The question's not relevant. The only thing I'm interested in is the science.
He turns back to his work. We hear the door close as Diamond leaves.

A GEODESIC DOME
White, space-age, is being erected on the lawn. Workmen are unloading the
NASA trucks. We pull back through a high window of the Biology building. A woman
stands there, looking out. Her name is KRIS McQUADE. This is her office -

MCQUADE

You want to tell me what's going on?
She turns and looks at Diamond, sitting on the other side of the desk,

DIAMOND

Don't ask, Kris, I'd have to lie and I don't want to do that to my best friend,

MCQUADE

The rumor is, you've done something really big. They say the Defense
Department is taking it over.
Diamond just sits there, staring straight ahead. McQuade waits. Finally -

MCQUADE (CONT'D)

Okay, okay - I'm sorry I asked. So what about this guy - what's he done?

DIAMOND

He hasn't done anything - I'm just interested.

MCQUADE

Ten thousand employment records I've got on file and you want to know about a lab
assisant?

DIAMOND

The smartest assistant I've ever known.

MCQUADE

What - he can mop and fart at the same time?
She picks up pages from a computer printer - including a copy of Will's photo I.D.

MCQUADE (CONT'D)

He's handsome, at least I'll say -
(a thought strikes her)
Jesus - you're not interested in him like that, are you?

DIAMOND

No, but he's the most unbelievable smelling man.

MCQUADE

Smelling? You're pregnant - obviously your hormoncs have gone crazy. What exactly
does he smell like?

DIAMOND

You know...
(searching for the right word)
.., wholesome.

MCQUADE
Of course he does - that's the Lysol.
Diamond laughs but McQuade barely notices it. She's leafing through WiU's file -

MCQUADE (CONT'D)
That's strange - there's supposed to be a background sheet. Family, school
-all that shit. It must have gotten lost.
Before Diamond can say anything, a young man enters. He's McQuada's assistant.

ASSISTANT
Your secretary's on the line, Dr Diamond. There's a call for you.

DIAMOND
Tell her to take a message.

ASSISTANT
It's the New York Times.

MCQUADE
What do they want?

DIAMOND
I think Washington's news management just went south.

THE WHITE HOUSE
Night. Scores of television news vans are parked outsideDutch, Japanese and
French reporters are doing stand-ups live-to-air. We hear Peter Jennings of

ABC.
JENNINGS (O.S.)
We're standing by to go live to Washington as events continue to unfold on this
remarkable day. I don't think there's a person anywhere who's not sitting by a radio or
television now. I'm told the President is on his way to the press room -

FIFTH AVENUE is totally empty - just a young man on rollerblades. He skates
effortlessly down the deserted avenue - past Tiffany's and the Trump Tower, all silent
now.

PRESIDENT (O.S.)
My fellow Americans...
The rollerblader passes the cathedral of St John. The front doors are open.
Someone is playing the organ - Mozart's Requiem. The rollerblader fades into the night.

STEEL DOOR OPENS
A sharp-faced caretaker - scruffy clothes and a limp - escorts Will into a vaulted
basement. All we can see are silhouettestowers of crates, racks of equipment...

CARETAKER
This used to be the basement of the Psychology Department. We just sort of stacked everything around 'em -
He flicks a switch - the storage room floods with light. He points at two long iron cylinders - like small submarines - rigged up to a series of valves and pipes.

CARETAKER (CONT'D)
Flotation tanks. They used 'em for experiments in sensory degradation -

WILL
Deprivation - sensory deprivation.

CARETAKER
Yeah, well - whatever.

SHAFT OF LIGHT
WILL OPENS AN IRON HATCH THAT GIVES ACCESS INTO ONE OF THE TANKS. HE DROPS
INTO IT AND WALKS FORWARD, EXAMINING IT. THE DARKNESS CLOSES AROUND HIM. HE
STARES AHEAD. VOICES DRIFT OUT OF MEMORY -
YOUNG MAN (O.S.)
Now I know what a mole feels like -

YOUNG WOMAN (O.S.)
(lightly)
It feels like a fucking coffin, that's what it feels like.
Other voices laugh. They're all young and like the young they think they'll never die.

CARETAKER (O.S.)
Hey, fella - what are you doing?

HE'S PEERING DOWN THROUGH THE HATCH. WILL DRAGS HIMSELF OUT OF THE PAST. HE
TURNS -
WILL
Just looking. I'll be coming back - I'll need a key.
The caretaker shrugs - sure. Will climbs out of the tank.

WILL (CONT'D)
One other thing - don't tell anyone, huh?

CARETAKER
Who would I tell? They treat me like shit Worse than shit. All work, no appreciation. The phantom of Harvard. Someone should write a fucking musical about me.

CIRCLES OF LIGHT
Desk lamps, glowing in an office. Diamond and a team of researchers are working through piles of old journals and extracts from scientific papers.

RESEARCHER
Here's another one - "Mitochondrial DNAA Map to the Past."

DIAMOND
Who's it by?

RESEARCHER
Same guy - Doctor Robert Plant.

DIAMOND
Jesus, what did this guy do - write the book on it? Who is he?

HUGE BOOK BEING OPENED
It's a scientific directory. The researcher flicks the pages and stops at
"Plant".

RESEARCHER
Wow - I thought your career was impressive.
Diamond looks up from her reading.

RESEARCHER (CONT'D)
Degrees in medicine and microbiology. A PhD at 24, a member of the Academy of Sciences, published twenty times by 1974...

DIAMOND
And then?

RESEARCHER
Then nothing.

DIAMOND REACTS. SHE GETS TO HER FEET, COMING CLOSER -
DIAMOND
Where did he go as an undergraduate?

RESEARCHER
Princeton.

DIAMOND
On a scholarship?

A CORRIDOR

It's late at night. The scientists and their staff are working around the clock. Will wheels a trolley laden with bottles, vials, and catheters down a crowded corridor. Diamond pushes through the people behind, trying to catch up to him. Scientists turn to speak to her but she ignores them.

DIAMOND (CONT'D)
Robert!
Will keeps walking, heading for an elevator. Diamond skirts around a knot of people.

DIAMOND (CONT'D)
Doctor Plant!
Will hesitates - one split second - then keeps going. The elevator doors slide open. Will steps in, turns and hits a button. He watches Diamond pushing towards him. For a moment their eyes meet. She comes closer.
Sswhish! The doors slide shut.

DIAMOND'S OFFICE
She sits behind her desk, listening to the chief of campus security.

SECURITY OFFICER
The equipment you saw him with was taken from three labs. It includes a range of genetic material-
(hands her an inventory)
We've checked all the buildings your team is using - he's not in any of them.

DIAMOND
What about hie house?

SECURITY OFFICER
He asked his landlady to look after his cat. She hasn't seen him for three days.

IN THE BASEMENT there's a make-shift bed and a hot-plate with a battered saucepan. Next to it is a rack of medical equipment and laboratory vials.
Will is sit'ting in front of three computers running in parallel - data and equations reel across them. The caretaker comes out of the shadows, carrying two mugs of thick coffee. He puts one down next to Will -

CARETAKER
You wanna tell me what exactly you're doing?

WILL
Looking for a date.
The caretaker stares at the confusion of diagrams and equations on the screen -

CARETAKER
What's wrong with a calendar?

WILL
These are chemical sequences - they represent human genes. By following a trail of mutations, I can date them. I'm trying to find out when a major change occurred in something called the mitochondrial DNA.

CARETAKER
The mitochondrial DNA? Yeah... well that makes sense.
But Will barely hears it. Suddenly he's leaning forward, keyboarding in complex commands. The caretaker watches him -

CARETAKER (CONT'D)
You've found it?

WILL
Maybe...
He has illustrations of two long-chain molecules on the screen. He moves them together. Aa they overlap, we see they're not identical - the tail of one kicks upwarda. Will starel at it -

WILL (CONT'D)
(softly)
Yeah - I've found it.

CARETAKER
So - what's the date?
Will presses a key. Faster than the eye can follow, the first long-chain molecule starts to shift and mutate. Finally it resolves itself into the second molecule. Will looks at a graph on the side of the screen -

WILL
The best computer science can do? One hundred and two thousand years ago.

CARETAKER
Sort of what I figured - give or take a day or two.

DIAMOND'S OFFICE
Diamond is poring through scientific articles written by Will. She flicks a page -there's a photo of Will, 20 years younger, surrounded by three colleagues. He's got his arm around one of them - an attractive young woman.
Diamond lifts the photo, looking at it more closely. She starts to read the caption. We push in on it and hold on the words... "UC Berkeley".

WE ARE FLYING swooping and soaring - through a weird landscape of towering cliffs, tumbling streams and primordial forest. There's something unreal about it - we pull back to reveal they're computer-generated images, playing on the screens in the basement.

The caretaker has pulled up a chair. He and Will are watching the images generated by a CD-ROM.

WILL
This is someone's version of the prehistoric world. I'm interested in the geography, the atmosphere -that sort of stuff.

CARETAKER
Where are we?

WILL
Africa - that's where Mankind started.
Will keeps looking at the strange images. The caretaker gets to his feet -

CARETAKER
I'll see you in the morning.

WILL
Yeah.
The caretaker limps towards the door. Will looks up -

WILL (CONT'D)
Thank you - for helping me, I mean.

CARETAKER
It sounds like you're leaving or something.

WILL
No. I just wanted to say it, that's all.
The caretaker keeps looking at him -

CARETAKER
What exactly are you doing? You're a bit old to try and make your mark, aren't you? Anyway, nobody listens to people like us.

WILL
Fate can be kind - sometimes a man gets a second chance. Do you know what it's like to be ridiculed, to have your ideas thrown back in your face? And that was the easy part. I guess that's what I'm doing - I want to prove that I was right.

CARETAKER
You're lying to me.

WILL

What do you mean?!

CARETAKER
You are going somewhere. I don't know where it is. I'm not even sure I can imagine it.
Good luck, though. I hope you find whatever it is you're looking for.

WILL
Thanks.

CARETAKER
No point in getting you breakfast, huh?
Will shakes his head - no. They smile at each other. The caretaker turns and goes.

DIAMOND'S OFFICE
Diamond looks up from the papers and articles littering her desk. Her
Secretary stands in the doorway -

SECRETARY
I've got Eleanor Wilkins on the phone. She runs the archives at Berkeley.

DIAMOND
(into phone)
Ms Wilkins?
We push in tight on Diamond's face as she listens. Anxiety and alarm register on it.

OUTER OFFICE
The security officer and several of his men are looking at maps of the campus.
Researchers and scientists have gathered in the office, rumors are flying. Everyone turns
- Diamond stands in the doorway to her office. She looks at deMaupassant.

DIAMOND (CONT'D)
You were right, Luc. That work you remembered from Berkeley - he was the one that
did it. He said man was the last step on an evolutionary trail.
Within every one of us is the history of our race. It's imprinted on our genes - like a
map. Anyone that can find the chemical key can travel back down it. Through the womb.
Through time and space -
(she looks at them all)
That's what he's doing. He's going back. He's going to try and change evolution.

SECURITY OFFICER
Is that possible?

DIAMOND
He was the best of his generation. He thinks so. He's got the genetic material for the
key. All he needs are flotation tanks.

THE FLOTATION TANKS

The valves are open - warm water is pouring into the tanks.
Will sits next to the rack of medical equipment, beads of sweat on his forehead. He slides a syringe into his forearm and inserts a catheter. He opens a series of tiny valves on the glass vials. A cocktail of fluid - minutely measured doses - flows down the clear plastic towards his arm. The fluid hits his blood stream and drains into it.

A LONG CORRIDOR

Diamond and the others run fast through pools of light cast by naked bulbs.
Ahead -a pair of swing doors -

BOB

A theory's one thing - do you really think he'll try it?

DIAMOND

He's spent fifteen years as a lab assistant. He lives in a two room walk-up with a cat. No family, no friends. What's There's left for him here? Of course he'll do it.
Smack! They push through the doors, into another corridor.

AN IRON LADDER

Will climbs up the side of the flotation tank. Suddenly he stops - a tremor, a rippling wave, passes from his feet to his head. It's his muscles contracting. It wracks him with pain. He gasps at the intensity of it.
Smash! The steel door into the basement shudders as someone tries to get in. Will looks up - the door twists and moves. His vision is starting to distort. He grabs the access hatch and swings through -
Splashl He drops into the water. Clang! He closes the hatch.
Barn? The steel door flies open. The security officer lowers a sledge hammer. Diamond steps in end throws a light switch.

DARKNESS IN THE TANK

Will floats on his back, the only sound is the rapid thump of his heartbeat. The water sloshes back and forth - his muscles are going into spasms. We push along his body - up to his face. His eyes roll back into his headl
All we see are the whites of them. They shatter into a web of capillaries -

WILL'S POV red mist swirls in front of him. It resolves itself into a web of interwoven tendrils -the double helix of the DNA molecule. Will starts to travel through it -

INSIDE THE TANK

Will is morphing, shedding cells - we're losing him in the warm, dark fluid of the tank. It's like the womb. His body seems to be disintegrating, dissolving into it. Water flows through the sockets where his eyes once were.
His hollow mouth opens. From far away we hear him scream - a primal scream.

OUTSIDE THE TANK

Not a sound escapes. The security officer is about to try and open the hatch.

DIAMOND (O.S.)
NO!
The security officer turns - Diamond is holding the catheter in her hand.

DIAMOND (CONT'D)
If we open the hatch, I think we'll kill him. It's too late - it's his journey, he's going to have to take it.

INSIDE THE TANK
Will's body is like a shadow, almost one with the water, growing less distinct by the moment. What is left of his face - a strange, shifting shape - floats towards us. Closer... closer. It melts completely into the water -

WILL'S POV
He spirals down a tunnel - into a whirlpool of white light. As he hits, it shatters into a million fragments of light. It looks like a comet, wheeling through the heavens. A cosmic wind blows it forward. Will is traveling through space and time -

OUTSIDE THE TANK
Diamond and the others are gathered around the computers. Bob is working the keyboard. Diamond is looking.through the piles of papers, notes and star charts.

DIAMOND
Everything's here - he kept a record of every step. He can even tell the date -forty hours after he arrives there's a solar eclipse.

BOB
Billie - there's a note for you.
Diamond looks over his shoulder at the computer screen. She reads what is writ'ten -

DIAMOND
"I won't be here, but if I solve this thing make sure you tell them,
Billie. Tell them it was Robert Plant, Doctor Robert Plant of UC Berkeley."

THE FRAGMENTS OF LIGHT blaze through the heavens. They draw together, changing and reconstituting into a shape we recognize - the interwoven strands of DNA molecules. The strands connect. A blast of light! It's the rays of -

THE SUN streaming into a cave. Will lies in the fetal position, bleeding from his nose and ears. The light grows stronger - it's dawn. Will drags himself up and stumbles towards the entrance. We tilt up from him. He doesn't see it, but we do - prehistoric cave paintings are etched into the rock.

A CRAGGY PEAK

Will steps out of the cave. Sunrise sweeps over a world born brand new - plains and jungle and primordial forest. Rising above it is a snow-capped mountain that looks like Kilamlnjlro. A ragged gash runs across the earth - a rift valley. Will stares at it. He raises his face to the sun. He did it.
The first step's over - and he did itl He looks down - rising out of the valley is a tiny pillar of smoke.

A FOREST CLEARING
In the middle are the smoldering remains of a camp-fire. Will moves cautiously towards it. He stops - several bodies, terribly mangled, lie on the ground.
Will turns one of them over - he's got matted hair, a heavy brow and a short, muscular body. As primitive as he is, there's no doubt of his species. He is a man. A Paleolithic man.
This was a hunting party -scattered weapons and the trussed carcasses of dead animals lie nearby. For a moment Will thinks the hunters must have been torn apart by wild animals. Then he looks up into the trees - more bodies of the hunters. But no animal did this - they hang from iron chains, left there as some sort of trophy. Or a warning.

CRUSHED LEAVES AND BROKEN PLANTS
Will is following a tiny trail through the forest. He's taken what is useful from the bodies of the hunters - an otter-skin water bag, two short-handled spears and a bed-roll made from an animal pelt. He moves on - deeper into the shadows of the forest.

A SPARKLING STREAM
Will splashes through the crystal water. He looks upstream - a small lake.
A flock of strange birds - like huge flamingos take flight in a blaze of pink and gold.
He steps out of the stream and along a path beneath a canopy of over-arching trees. We hold on his feet - whip! He triggers something. A net of woven vines engulfs him. He drops the spears and bedroll. Suddenly he's soaring through the air.
He jerks to a halt - he's a netted animal hanging high in the trees. The faces of two Paleolithic men, crouched on boughs, stare at him.

PLUME OF WATER cascades a hundred feet into a hidden gorge. Smoke curls up from fires.
Scores of stone-age people - man, women and children - turn and look. Will, roped and bound, is being hauled into the encampment.
The primitive people - nervous but intrigued - circle around him. They are dressed in skins and fur. talismans hang from their necks. The warriors carry not only weapons but ritual scars across their foreheads. It makes them look even more savage.
Will is led past the haunches of soma massive animal cooking in a pit. A pile of ivory tusks lie nearby. The two captors jerk on the leash - it stops Will in front of a cave. Hanging from the roof is the giant pelt and head of their totema saber-toothed tiger. This is the Tribe of the Tiger.
A man emerges from under its outstretched paws. He's in his late 20's - proud and strong. His name is Kip-Kena - he is their leader. He and Will look at one another.

Kip uses his hands to sign to Will in the formal language of his race. Will stares at him - he has no idea what it means. He shrugs. Kip tries a new tack - he speaks. The sounds are rough and guttural - but understandable,

KiP Where is your tribe?

Will pauses, searching for an answer- where do you start? He gives up.

WILL
I don't have a tribe.
A rolling murmur of disbelief from the surrounding tribe.

KIP
No man can live without a tribe! How would he hunt the mighty animals? Who would keep his fire burning?

WILL
I come from far away... I'm a traveler.

KIP
What is traveler? Is that a tribe?
Again Will's at a loss. Something catches Kip's eye. He reaches forward and rips the water bag out from under Will's coat. The tribe reacts -

KIP (CONT'D)
You carry things taken from our hunters! Kill him.
He turns away. Will throws himself at him -

WILL
NO!
Whackl A blow to the back of Will's neck knocks him to his knees. He looks up -two warriors have their spears raised, about to plunge them into his chest.
A sound like thunder - it's hooves. The warriors turn. Will follows their gaze - half an army, mounted on horseback, surges into the gorge, They are heavily armed, dressed in armor but it's not their weaponry that astonishes
Will. These are apes!
The tribes-people scream in terror. They turn and run. The two warriors forget about Will. He dives for cover in a pile of rocks. As he tears himself free of the ropes that bind him, he looks out -
The apes charge in to the camp. At their head is a huge gorillarippling muscles and intelligent eyes - deep set and yellow, like pissholes in the snow. He wears a suit of black armor ribbed in silver. His name is Drak. He is the Lord of the High Rivers, supreme commander of the ape army. On either side ride his elite Praetorian Guard.
Woo-woo-woo! Kip swings a hollow piece of wood above his head. It's a bull-roarer. The warriors of the tribe know its meaning - they rally to
Kip's side. Armed only with spears and primitive bows they stand between the apes and their panic-driven people, trying to buy them time to get into the cave.
Sswhish! The sound of arrows. The apes carry triple-barreled iron crossbows.

Short iron bolts cut several of the tribesmen down. Dust and smoke swirls across the camp. Kip and his men, fighting all the way, retreat towards the cave.

A baby's cry! Will turns - a toddler sits at a hearth, left behind in the confusion. Will half rises to his feet, about to go for him. Too late - there's a blur of movement irt the trees. A tribe-boy - too young to be a warrior - has come back for the child.

Out of the dust and smoke - Drak! Foam flies from his horse's mouth. He's seen the boy and the child. He locks what looks like a Gatling gun tight under his huge bicep.

Will screams a warning. The boy turns - he sees Drak as he fires. A hail of iron darts - twenty or more - cut him and the child down.

Rage flashes in Will's eyes. He scrambles over a boulder and rips a crossbow from a dead ape's hand. He slides bolts into the barrels and grabs a lever with both hands -you need the strength of an ape to cock it. A sound behind him - little more than a whisper. He swings -It's an arrow.

Whackl It rips into his shoulder, hurling him to the ground. Ape infantry - foot soldiers - are coming into the gorge behind him.

In their midst are three huge steam-driven machines - like iron erector sets. One is the Claw, one is the Balls and the other is the Flame.

THE CAVE ENTRANCE

Kip and his warriors have seen them too. They scramble into the cave. Men and women are inside, swinging closed two huge stockade doors made from tree trunks.

Other warriors, caught outside, run for the closing gap. On their heels is Will - still clutching the crossbow, blood streaming from his wound. The doors are closing... closing. Will dives through the gap, almost crushed -

INSIDE THE CAVE

Slam! The doors fly shut. Wham! A huge cross-beam drops into place. Will, sprawled in the dust, looks up - chaos. By torchlight, the medicine man is tending the wounded, children are screaming, women and old people are clambering up a series of ledges. High above is a tiny slash of daylightanother entrance.

From deep in the cave Will hears the roar of some animal but he doesn't have time to think about it. Smash! The great wooden doors shudder from some mighty blow.

OUTSIDE THE DOORS

The three machines are in place. The first of them has two huge stone balls suspended by chains from an overhead jib. An ape sits right on top, operating it. The balls dance and swing wildly - smash! They hit the door, opening a hole.

INSIDE THE CAVE

Daylight streams in. Kip and his warriors have ranged themselves high around the walls, ready to attack when the apes pour in. A pair of huge iron jaws appear in the hole. This is the second of the apes' machines - the Claw.

Another roar from the animal. Will watches the Claw reach in and grab the massive crossbeam. It snaps it like a twig. Will gets to his feet and runs.

He sees Kip signal -

AN OLD WARRIOR is perched high on a series of wooden bars that seal off a corner of the cave, turning it into a cage. He opens it.

Crash! The stockade doors at the front of the cave burst open. The first of the ape cavalry charges in. A roar from the unseen animal. The apes' horses catch the scent of it. They whinny in terror.

Will stares as a blur of striped fur and muscle flies out of the cage. The tribe's totem is a living thing - the saber-toothed tiger ia three times the size of its Bengal cousin, a head the size of an ox and two ten-inch teeth curved down either side of its jaw.

The horses are bucking and rearing. The tiger leaps towards the door, heading for freedom. A dismounted ape raises his weapon. The tiger doesn't even break stride. One lazy swipe from his paw tears open the armor and flesh of the ape's chest.

Will can smell the animal's breath as it flies past. An ape officer, still on his horse, turns - another swipe from the.tiger's paw rips out his throat.

Kip and his warriors hurl their spears and stone tomahawks at the cavalry - half of them dismounted, all of them in disarray. The tiger runs soars through the doorway -

OUTSIDE THE CAVE

Drak fights to control his mount as the tiger lands once and bounds into the forest.

ON THE LEDGES

Kip's men are fighting as they retreat, heading towards the opening at the roof of the cave. Will, clutching his wounded shoulder, makes his own way up the wall.

Beneath him, Drak and the apes roll in the third of the machines - a long iron tube in a rolling superstructure. Feeding it are a series of oil-filled bladders. One of the apes touches a torch to a firing hole. A tongue of fire erupts from the end of the tube. It's a flame thrower -The fiery tongue shoots up towards the roof of the cave. The flame engulfs two warriors. Skin blazing, they plummet to the ground.

The flame thrower fires again - scorching the rock wall, filling the cave wit a pall of smoke. It hits the tiny patch of daylight, cutting off escape.

Will - trapped - runs along a ledge, over a pile of rocks and jumps. Into mid-air! He lands on the back of a riderless horse and drives his heels into its flanks.

The apes and the surviving warriors turn. For a moment they just stare - nobody's ever seen a human ride a horse before. Will flies towards the entrance. He sees Kip on a ledge just above, battling three huge apes.

WILL

Jump!

Kip sees Will galloping towards him. One of the apes raises a double-bladed sword. Kip jumps sprawling across the horse's neck, grabbing on to its flowing mane.

Drak stares at Will - he's never seen anything like him. He wheels his horse around and spurs it forward in pursuit.

OUTSIDE THE CAVE

Will's horse bursts out of the cave - past the Claw and under the Balls.

The apes turn and look - astonished. They scramble for their horses. Drak charges through.

Will hurtles towards the trees. Kip, hanging on for life, looks behind -
Drak raises his Gatling gun and aims. Kip wrenches Will's head down - zing!
The arrows skim past.
Drak can't outpace them - and he can't re-load at the gallop either. They charge out of the camp, into -

THE DAPPLED LIGHT OF THE FOREST
Drak rises up in the stirrups and hauls himself on to the saddlethe huge ape stands on the back of the charging horse!
He jumps - his rippling arms catch hold of an overhanging bough. He swings himself up into the tree - he is an ape, after all. He throws himself from branch to bough, traveling at incredible speed.
Will glances back - he sees Drak's riderless horse. His eyes dart in confusion -where is he? We crane up - he's in the trees above! Drak jumps -
Wham! Hundreds of pounds of gorilla blast into Will's shoulder, lifting him out of the saddle and hurling him to the ground.
Kip hauls down on the horse's bridle - wheeling the stallion around.
Will looks up from the dust - Drak towers above him. Will sees Kip coming back -

WILL (CONT'D)
Run!
A volley of arrows whiz past Kip - other apes are galloping through the trees. Kip grabs the bridle and kicks - the horse spins and gallops away. massive, armor-clad paw grabs Will's head. He looks straight into Drak's face. The ape reaches out and rips a claw down Will's cheek. Will tries to stifle the scream. Drak touches the wound and tastes the blood
-

DRAK
So - it's human, after ell.
He spits the blood out in revulsion. Will stares into the piu-holes in his face. Never has he seen eyes so cold.
Will tries to rise to hie feet. His wounded shoulder has weakened him - he staggers.
Drak's clenched fist, clad in chain mail, drives straight et
Will's jaw. Smashl Fade to black.

THE WORLD UPSIDE DOWN
It's Will's point of view - he-s lying on his back in a horse-drawn cart.
He's very weak, his shirt drenched in blood. He rolls over and the image rights itself.
He drags himself on to all fours but he can't get any further - his lcgs are chained.

WILL
(fevered, disoriented)
Where the fuck am I?
Will looks up - a huge ape sits guard in the back of the wagon.

GUARD

(smiling)
The end of the road.
Will - confused, panicky - grabs the side of the cart and hauls himself to his knees. He
looks past an escort of ape cavalry - they are traveling down an avenue of idols -
towering statues of apes, sculpted out of stone, old as ages past. Fires burn somewhere
within them giving the eyes a red, flickering glow.
Will turns away. Behind him he sees humans, rows of them - dead - hanging upsidl
down from long poles like trophies.
Everything comes flooding back - he slumps against the side of the cart, eyes barely
focused. Blood trickles down under his shirt and forms a pool between his legs. He
doesn't even notice it.

MASSIVE IRON AND WOOD BRIDGE spans a roaring river. Drak and his convoy
clatter across it. We crane up - laid out before is a city. Terraces are cut into both sides
of a jagged ravine. Opening on to them are caves and houses and buildings made out of
stone.
Apes are everywhere - hammering stones to enlarge a house, chattering in the trees,
swinging hand-over-hand along horizontal ladders - crossing from one side of the ravine
to the other.
Will has roused himself. He stares at the city through feverish eyes - to him, it appears
to float. Buildings swim in and out of focus. His shoulders shake - he starts to laugh, an
edge of hysteria to it.

WILL
A city... of course. Ape city! I've destroyed my mind. Or maybe I'm dead and this is
God's last joke - hell is ruled by apes.
Whhish - the end of a whip sails through the air. Crack! It hits Will's back, doubling
him over.

GUARD
Quiet, animal!

RIPPLES OF WATER run across the surface of a beautiful pool. A black shape glides
along underwater. The head breaks the surface - it's an old gorilla, the fur on his face
gray and balding. This is NAZGUL. He is the Ghan - the President - of the Council of
Elders.
He walks out of the water. Other old apes - all male, their days of warring and building
over - lie around the pool. Several of them, draped only in rough loin-cloths, groom
each other, picking nits out of their fur.
The sound of a gong! Nazgul picks up a loin cloth and walks the end of the pool. He
looks straight down the ravine - at the far end, Drak and his troop come into view.

NAZGUL
The raiders are home.

OLD APE

(lazily)
Good hunting?
Nazgul squints against the sun. He sees the poles carrying the dead humans.

NAZGUL
By the look of it.

**GRAY-BEARDED WARRIOR, HIS CHEST MARKED BY THE SCARS OF MANY BATTLES, GETS
UP -**
GRAY BEARD
(proudly)
Not as good as when we rode the high ridges, I'll warrant.

NAZGUL
Times are different now. Back then, a could go out and come back with a brace of animals. They're far scarcer now -

OLD APE
Not scarce enough, I say.
There's a murmur of agreement from the other apes.

A TINY BOAT is wreathed in woven leaves. Lying in it is the dead body of a young ape.
The boat drifts down an underground stream. All around it rise the stone walls of a huge cavern. Torches light up the gloom - this place is a temple.
A group of apes - mourners - walk along a path, keeping pace with the funeral boat.
They make a humming sound deep in the back of their throats - a dirge for the dead.
At the head of the procession, swinging a smoking censer, is an ape wearing a lion-skin cloak. His face is scarred and twisted - he has one cruel eye, the other is just an empty socket. Beneath the cloak, one arm and a leg are withered. The whole effect, rather than diminishing his power, enhances it.
His name is MA-GOG. He is high priest of the apes, defender of the faith, keeper of the Book of the Lore.
The funeral boat gathers speed in the current. It thrusts towards sunlight pouring through an arch.

A ROCK PLATFORM
The mourners step through the arch and on to a slab of rock. We pull back to reveal where they stand - a huge crouching ape has been carved out of the face of a cliff, Its bowed front legs form the archway, the entrance to the temple of the ape.

**CLOUDS OF MIST AND WIND-BLOWN SPRAY SWEEP OVER MA-GOG AND THE MOURNERS. ALL
AROUND THEM, THE SOUND OF ROARING WATER. THE FUNERAL BOAT FLOATS OUT OF THE**

TEMPLE AND INTO A ROARING RIVER. MA-GOG SWINGS THE CENSER OVER THE WATER -

MA -GOG
(intoning)
In the beginning was the word, and the word was the Book of the Lore. It says God created the ape in His own image. Alone among His creatures, the ape has a soul. One crosses the river now but death is only a door. He will dwell in the house of the Lord forever. Amen The mourners beat their chests with their fists. They repeat the word "Amen".
For a moment the clouds of mist clear. Now we see where the boat is headed - half an ocean of water pours over a sheer drop. These are the Falls of No Return. The boat races forward - over the waterfall it goes.
The sound of cheering voices, very faint, drifts towards them. Ma-Gog turns and looks up the river towards the city -

APES HANG FROM THE 'LADDERS' looking down on Drak and his troops. The convoy passes along a road cut into the side of the ridge. Apes have come out of the houses and buildings to greet them.
Will lies in the back of the cart, unconscious. Faces of apes stare in at him - they've never seen anything like it. A young ape - a little boy - stands with his grandfather.

KID
What is it?

GRANDFATHER
Some... sort of human.

KID
But look at the eyes, 'Pa - they're the color of the sea. Where's it from?

GRANDFATHER
I don't know - a traveler, maybe. Nobody knows what lies beyond the Tower of the Moon.

THE WORD "TRAVELER" IS PICKED UP BY OTHER APES. IT RIPPLES THROUGH THE CROWD. A WOMAN ON THE OTHER SIDE OF THE WAGON CALLS OUT -

WOMAN
No it's not - it's a mutant.

LABORER
Put it in the zoo!
A female ape pushes them aside. She's heavy-set, bright eyes, an air of authority about her. Over her shoulder she carries a leather satchel with a series of steel instruments dangling from it. Her name is ZORA - she is a doctor.

She and her ASSISTANT - a young male - swing themselves on to the cart.
Kneeling beside him, Zora puts her hand down and grabs hold of Will's crotch.

ZORA
Whatever it is, it's male.
She rips open Will's shirt - his chest is covered in blood from the gaping wound.

ZORA (CONT'D)
Probe.
The Assistant hands her a steel instrument. She slides it towards the wound. We hold
on Will's face - a strangled cry but he doesn't regain consciousness. Zore returns the
bloodied probe to her Assistant. She calls out -

ZORA (CONT'D)
Drak!
The leader of the ape warriors, riding close by, turns -

ZORA (CONT'D)
The animal's bleeding to death, my Lord.
Drak rides up to the wagon.

DRAK
I didn't bring him all this way just to have him die.

ZORA
(to the assistant)
Ben-Guri - get a vet. Quicklyl

AN APE IN A LEATHER APRON uses a grinding wheel to sharpen a gruesome
looking knife. This is the VET.
Will lies on a stone slab nearby - it's a sort of medical centersinks along the walls, racks
of equipment, hoses to wash down the blood.
The Vet cuts the clothing away from Will's wound. He turns to Doctor Zora -

VET
We're going to have to give him blood.

PRISONER IN A CELL
He's a tribesman - in his late 40s. Despite his tattered furs and hollow chccks, he carries
himself with dignity - he's a proud man. His name is
ARAGORN. On a chain around his neck he wears a metal ornament, like crescent
moon. Etched into it are strange markings and the totems of various tribes.
The sound of a key in lock. Aragorn turns - the cell door is thrown back.
Three ape guards enter. Two of them, armed with spears, drive Aragorn into a corner.
The third ape has a leather collar on the end of a pole. He drops it over Aragorn's head.
Aragorn struggles but the ape jerks the collar tight. They drag him from the cell.

TEAM OF HORSES

- their flanks drenched in sweat - walk in a circle. They turn a huge wheel that controls a series of pulleys and winches. Attached to the end of a heavy cable is a wooden platform - a primitive elevator. It runs from a series of impressive house, down the side of the ravine, to the center of the city.

Standing on the platform are Nazgul and several other elders. They look down on the central square. It's crowded with apes - soldiers are being greeted by their kin.

ARAGORN LIES ON HIS BACK

He's strapped to a slab, half-naked, in the medical center. They've put a gag in his mouth and though he struggles to free himself, he can barely move.

Will, still unconscious, lies on a table next to him. Nazgul peers down at him.

NAZGUL

It's human, you say?

Doctor Zora nods - yes.

NAZGUL

It's even uglier than the others.

He pulls a covering aside and looks at Will's naked legs.

NAZGUL (CONT'D)

How can he hunt with legs like those -they're like twigs. Maybe he's diseased.

Everybody shrugs - who knows?

The Vet heats a steel needle over an open flame. The other end of the needle is attached to a length of animal intestine. It acts as a tube. The

Vet grabs Will's forearm and slides the red-hot needle into the vein.

Will's body jerks with the pain. Nazgul and the others spring back.

For a moment Will's wrenched back to consciousness - he sees a light-filled room, a bandage on his chest, a bladder full of blood hanging above him.

His puts it together the only way he knows - he thinks he's in hospital

WILL

(groggy)

Help me. I've got health insurance. Honest...

His eyes close as he slips back into darkness. Nazgul looks at Doctor Zora.

NAZGUL

What is health insurance?

DOCTOR ZORA

Some sort of religion...?

The Vet turns and makes an adjustment to the bladder. Another length of tubing snakes out of it and is attached by a needle to Aragorn's arm. It's his blood. Now we realize - this is the ape version of a blood transfusion.

NAZGUL
Do you think this'll work?

VET
You can never tell with animals. Their bodies aren't as sophisticated as an ape's. Sometimes their blood fights with each other. Either way, you know really quick -they get up and walk around, or they're dead.
The Vet turns a little tap - Aragorn's blood flows down the tube. It hits
Will's vein.

WORDS CHISELED INTO STONE
"An Ape without knowledge is a fire without light."
Euripadape III
It stands over the doorway of a building high on a ridge. This is the Hall of Learning.
Ma-Gog - his lion skin cloak billowing behind him - hurries up the steps.

THE BLADDER OF BLOOD is empty. Guards are collaring Aragorn, preparing to drag him out. The door into the room is thrown open. Ma-Gog enters. Nazgul and the others greet him but he barely acknowledges it *

MA-GOG
Show him to me.
The Vet grabs Will's hair. He lifts up his head so that Ma-Gog can see his face.
The high priest takes a step back - there's something about Will that fills him with loathing. Anger flashes in his one good eye. He stares at Will.
His voice is Iow, almost to himself -

MA-GOG (CONT'D)
All my life I've dreaded this day.
(turns to the others)
Kill him.

DOCTOR ZORA
We've just spent an hour trying to save him -

MA-GOG
Kill him!
He grabs the stand holding the bladder and throws it to the ground. Doctor
Zora takes his arm, stopping him -

DOCTOR ZORA
The animal's unique, my lord. At least we should look at his brain. Maybe it's possible to remove the frontal lobes without killing him. Imagine - a tame human!

MA-GOG

Man can't be tamed. Alone among God's primates he kills for lust or greed.
He will murder his own brother to possess his brother's land.

NAZGUL
The doctor's only asking for a chance to experiment. The benefits would be enormous.
A tame species of human could double food production, at last we could dam the rivers.

MA-GOG
You don't know what you're dealing with.

NAZGUL
It's just an animal, Ma-Gog.

MA-GOG
It's not. That's the trouble.
A movement on the stone slab. They turn and look - Will's eyelids are fluttering. He's starting to come round. itl
He turns to Nazgul In the name of God - summon the Council of Elders.
Will's eyes are open now. Like through a glass - darkly - he sees the ape guards coming for him. He tries to struggle but he's very weak. They haul him off.

HEAVY IRON DOOR set in a rock wall - on one side a key-hole. We tilt up the door to a narrow set of bars high above it. A face, straining with effort, rises up to peer through the bars. It is Will - looking like death but forcing himself to do it, desperate to see where he is.

INSIDE THE CELL
The muscles across his shoulders ripple. His one good hand clutches the bars. He hangs by it, supporting his weight, staring out at a vaulted underground cavern. It looks like a cattle-yard, broken down and disused nowa series of long pens, wooden chutes and a primitive conveyor belt.
Will can't support himself any longer - he tumbles to the ground. He crawls across the floor and examines the door. It fits tight to the rock. There's no hope of picking the lock - the key-hole doesn't even come all the way through.
Suddenly he stops. Nothing for a moment, then he hears it again - a scraping sound.
He peers under the wooden bed at the stone blocks that form wall. One of the blocks moves. Will grabs hold of it and hauls it into the cell. Aragorn squeezes through from the adjoining cell. He looks at Will -

ARAGORN
So you lived, then?

WILL
What did they do?

ARAGORN

They gave you blood.
He holds up his bandaged forearm - Will realizes where it came from.

WILL
I hope you had a medical.
Aragorn looks at him - confused. From a distance, the sound of horses whinnying.

WILL (CONT'D)
What is this place?

ARAGORN
It was a slaughterhouse.

WILL
For horses?

ARAGORN
They use it for stables now. No - s different kind of animal. For humans.
Will stares, taken aback. Aragorn starts to gather twigs from the corners of the cell.

ARAGORN (CONT'D)
In my father's time, the apes rounded up tribes and brought them here.
Young apes killed some during their manhood rites, the others were made sport of in the corrals. At the end, the bodies were thrown onto the belts and fed to the fire.
Aragorn has made a pyramid of twigs and leaves. From out of his cloak, he takes two pieces of flint and strikes them. A spark starts the fire -

ARAGORN (CONT'D)
(softly)
Death is stuck to these walls, stranger -sounds not even s thousand winters can take away. Sometimes of s night they speak to me - I can hear the screams of my people.
Will looks at him. Firelight plays across their faces.

WILL
Why haven't they killed you?

ARAGORN
They keep me ss bait. My name is Aragorn -
He lifts his hand to Will - palm outwards. It's some form of greeting. Will returns it.

ARAGORN (CONT'D)
I am the Ranger of the Easterlings, the Leader of the Seven Tribes. They hope the warriors will come and try to free me.

WILL
And will they?

ARAGORN
Not if they fear my anger. I was taken in summer and now winter's almost gone. Even the apes grow tired - soon they'll make me walk the Paths of the
Dead.
Will looks at Aragorn's eyes - they're fearless. The ornament glints on his chest. Will points at it -

WILL what is it?

ARAGORN
It's called the Crescent of Light - it's the talisman of my rank.

WILL
Silver.

ARAGORN
Mithral is how we name it..
Will reaches his hand towards it -

WILL
Can I borrow it?
Aragorn recoils - this is the most precious thing in the world to him. His hand closes around the insignia -

ARAGORN
Who are you? What brings you to the valley of the tribes?

WILL
I meant you no harm. I'm looking for woman, one of my own kind. Do you know of people like me?

ARAGORN
Never.
Will nods his head, accepting it. Slowly he reaches his hand out -

WILL
If you want to get out of hare. I need the talisman. Aragorn.
The two men look at each other. A beat - then Aragorn reaches up and unfastens it.

THE TEMPLE OF THE APE
Torches burn on the walls. They cast a glow across the temple - the underground stream, pools of water, shelves of rock hewn out of the walls.
Several apes crouch on them, praying to a golden idol of an ape.
Mist rises off of the pools. Moving through it, we see Nazgul, Drak and e group of old apes. The Council of Elders is gathering. They pass through a narrow door -

THE TEMPLE'S INNER CHAMBER
Oil lamps - hidden in alcoves - illuminate Ma-Gog. He stands in front of an ancient book - strange symbols, like Sanskrit, run across its pages. This is the Book of the Lore. Ma-Gog looks at the Council of Elders seated in front of himNazgul, Drak and five other huge apes - all leaders in their time.

MA-GOG
How many scrolls are there in the Book of the Lore?
Nobody replies - the question is so obvious it needs no answer.

MA-GOG (CONT'D)
One-hundred-and-seventy-six, you say -every child knows that.
(softly)
But every child is wrong. There is one more scroll - the last scroll, sealed with seven seals, handed down from high priest to high priest...
He slides his hand under the top of the pedestal and releases a hidden catch. The top - the Book still resting on it - tilts up, revealing a secret compartment. It is lined with gold leaf. Lying in it is a slim folio of pages -

MA-GOG (CONT'D)
It is called the Scroll of Revelation.
The Council of Elders stare in awed silence. Ma-Gog takes the pages out and unfastens the seals. He reads -

MA-GOG (CONT'D)
"And it was given unto me to know the wisdom of ages. A silence fell and I saw a new heaven and a new earth. Like through a glass, darkly, I saw the future."
The Council of Elders stare at him. He limps forward and stops in front of them. He recites from memory -

MA-GOG (CONT'D)
"Behold - there rose out of the earth a pale horse and the name of the horse is Death. Those that ride on him are beasts, but like no beasts born before. Their limbs are weak but their eyes are as cold as the sea. They are given power over the earth to kill with the sword and with famine and with fire. And let him that hath understanding know the number of these beasts. It is the number of Man."
He raises his eyes and looks straight at the Councilors.

MA-GOG (CONT'D)
Today we saw that beast. Mark those words, my Lords - "their limbs are weak but they are given power over the earth". Now will you listen? Kill him!
And if we don't? Then all hope will fail in this bitter winter.
He lays down the secret scroll and closes the secret compartment. Nazgul looks from one to the other of the elders. Nobody says a word but he can read their grim expressions. He turns to Drek -

NAZGUL
Kill him. Kill him with the sword and with fire. Kill himl

THE KEYHOLE TO THE CELL
It's a shining bright image, slightly distorted. We pull back to reveal it's a reflection.
Aragorn's silver ornament has been polished to a brilliant luster. It's fixed to the end of
a length of wood sticking through the bars high above the iron door.

INSIDE THE CELL
The wooden bed has been smashed to pieces.
Both Aragorn and Will have used parts of their clothing to harness themselves so they
can see through the bars. Aragorn controls the pole with the "mirror" on the end of it.
By looking into it, Will can see the keyhole on the other side of the door.
He has a pole with a nail attached to the end of it. He turns the pole, guiding the nail
towards the keyhole. He's trying to pick the lock.

WILL
Do you understand time.., what time is it?
Aragorn looks at the shadows in the slaughterhouse -

ARAGORN
Seven hours since the rising of the sun.

WILL
Just after noon...

ARAGORN
Shouldn't we wait until night?

WILL
(concentrating)
If I'm right, it's gonna be dark a lot sooner than you think.
The nail is almost in the key-hole. Half an inch to go... a quarter. It slides off. Will
curses and starts again -

THE SUN beats down from a cloudleu sky. Drak and two huge Praetorian Guards -
Max and Hannibal - come through a huge stone portico. It's another entrance to the
Temple -one that opertl onto a central square. Orak and the two guards hurry across it.
towards the slaughterhouu.

THE NAIL at the end of the pole slides into the keyhole. Will - barely breathing in case
it breaks his concentration - listens carefully. He moves the end of the pole. The nail
turns.

HUGE SET OF DOORS are thrown open. Daylight spills into the slaughterhouse. Drak, Max and
Hannibal enter. Drak stops - he listens to the horses whinnying and stomping their hooves -

DRAK
Something's wrong!
(turns to Max)
Get the dogs.

HANNIBAL moves cautiously along the side one of the corrals, trying to see what's wrong with the horses. Behind him - a movement in the shadows.
Sswhish. The sound of something slicing through the air. He turns -
It's the side of Aragorn's hand. It chops hard into the ape's throat, shattering his larynx and blasting him into unconsciousness. He crumples to the ground.
Aragorn and Will strip him of his weapons. Will starts to go but Aragorn tears a strip off both their shirts. He ties the fabric around the ape's ankles.

WILL
What are you doing?

ARAGORN
Watch - they're going to bring in the dogs.

THE DOGS aren't really dogs at all - they're a much earlier ancestor. We call them wolves. There are two of them, on the end of heavy leather leashes. Their handlers have them in Will's cell, rubbing parts of the abandoned harnesses in front of their noses. The wolves take the scent.
Drak watches as the handlers unfasten the leashes. The wolves leap out of the cell.

HANNIBAL rises groggily to his feet, clutching his injured throat. He takes a few steps forward -Grrrr! He turns - the two wolves fly towards him. He tries to yell but the only sound he can make is a squeak.
He runs - the fabric, unseen by him, trails from his ankles. The wolves pound after him.
He glances over his shoulder. First one wolf - then the other - leaps.
Fangs and claws glistening, they hit him in the back, hurling him to the ground. He writhes on to his back. One wolf tears at his ankles, the other goes for his throat. Rip! Blood sprays as the artery breaks.

A STONE PASSAGE-WAY
Will and Aragorn are running, plunging down in to darkness. Arches and corridors open off of it. It's like a labyrinth -

WILL
This doesn't seem like the way out.

ARAGORN
We're not going out - not yet.

WILL STOPS, GRABBING HOLD OF HIM, TURNING HIM ROUND -
WILL
So what are we doing?

ARAGORN
(softly)
We're going killing.

WILL
Killing?! Don't be stupid -
Will jerks on Aragorn's arm, starting to haul him back. Aragorn throws off his hand -

ARAGORN
You do what you like! But I'm the Ranger of the Easterlings -I won't leave here until it's done.
From behind them - the sounds of pursuit.

WILL
Shit!
He starts to run. Together they disappear into the gloom ahead.

ROW OF CAGE-LIKE CELLS
Will and Aragorn glide past them. They're taking it slowly, very carefully.
Now we see why - ahead of them is a set of steel doors. Torches on either side illuminate a guard post but there's no sign of the sentry.
Will and Aragorn move closer. They pass -

CREVICE IN THE ROCK
We hold on the narrow opening, looking deep into the shadows. A big ape, heavily armed, stands there. He has his back to us, his legs spread. A trickle of water runs down the rock and drains away - he's taking a piss. A shadow flickers on the wall above him. He sees it -THE PASSAGE-WAYMore shadows -Will and Aragorn are move through the torchlight. The steel doors are straight ahead.
The sentry slides out of the crevice - he's behind Will. Silently, back pressed again6t the bars of a cell, he creeps closer to Will. He has a curved knife in one hand and a short-handled spear in the other. Closer... closer.
He raises the spear - a rustle of movement. Will spins - he sees the spear about to thrust. He's a dead man.
An arm? It shoots between the bars of the cell and locks around the sentry's throat, half choking him.
Will leaps forward and drives the butt of a weapon into the sentry's jaw.

The sentry crumples to the ground, revealing the face of the prisoner. It's not a man, though -it's an ape. He's in his prime - barrel chested and a fine head. His name is STRIDER.
He and Will look at each other through the bars.

STRIDER
Two rules in life - never play cards with anyone called Doc and never, whatever else you do, turn your back on an ape.
Will stares at him. Strider grins. Will smiles back -

WILL
Thanks. I'll remember that.
He starts to search the sentry.

ARAGORN
What are you doing?

WILL
Looking for the keys.

ARAGORN
No!

WILL
He saved our lives.

ARAGORN
He's an ape!
Will shrugs himself free of Aragorn's hand -

WILL
You go and kill as many apes as you like - I'm setting this one free.
Aragorn looks at him. A beat.

ARAGORN
(softly)
It's not apes I'm going to kill.

A PRISON LABORATORY
The heavy steel doors stand open. Inside is a clean and gruesome room - sinks and instruments along a wall, a series of operating tables and a row of cages.
Behind the bars are six tribes-people - men, women and a little boy. All of them carry surgical scars on their heads. It's made two of them blind; the others stare blankly into space.

Aragorn moves down the cages. Several of them shuffle towards him but there's no recognition - they're like the walking dead. Aragorn doesn't say a word. Grim-faced, he loads the crossbow and starts to fire, killing them.
Will and Strider come through the doorway - they see Aragorn going from cage to cage. Will steps forward, going to stop him. Strider's hand grabs his shoulder, restraining him.

STRIDER
Leave it. He knows what he's doing.
Will turns and looks at him, questioning.

STRIDER (CONT'D)
The doctors operate on them - up here.
(taps his head)
The tribes think that we steal their souls...
(he pauses - softly)
Maybe they're right.
Aragorn reaches the last cage. A woman - in her 20s - stands in the middle of the cell, looking at him. Aragorn stares at her face. His lip trembles with emotion. She tilts her head on one side, as if trying to work something out. Tears fill Aragorn's eyes. She stumbles a step forward. The
Ranger closes his eyes. He pulls the trigger. A crossbow bolt slams into her chest and she falls.
Will leans against the doorway, unwilling to watch, staring down the passageway. He turns at a footfall - Aragorn rejoins them. His voice is hollow, as if something has died within him -

ARAGORN
It's done. We can go now.
He turns and leads them back down the passageway.

THE WOLVES
There's five of them now, hunting through the slaughter-house in a pack.
All around them we see the torches of the apes as they search the nooks and crannies.
The horses whinny wildly as they catch the scent of the wolves.
Will, Aragorn and Strider are crouched in a corner of the corral, smearing their bodies with horse manure.

STRIDER
The fresher the better. Cover everything -that's the only way you'll hide your scent.
The wolves sniff the air, coming closer. Will, staring through the rungs of the coral, sees their gleaming eyes coming closer. He raises his crossbow, getting ready.
The wolves stop. They raise their heads and look - the whole cavern is growing dark. A giant shadow falls across the doorway into the outside world.
The horses rear and buck. The apes are staring - darkness is falling in the middle of the day. The wolves hackles rise in fear. They howl.
Aragorn and Strider are cowering back

ARAGORN
What is it?

WILL
Come on! Now!
He drags them forward and grabs hold of one of the horses.

AN UNEARTHLY LIGHT has fallen on the city. The apes are in confusion - soldiers and workers are running, children are screaming. A horse has thrown its rider and is bolting down the terraces.
The darkness grows ever deeper. In the sky, the face of the moon obliterates the sun - it's a full solar eclipse.
Two horses, flying at a gallop, charge through the doors of the slaughterhouse. Will is on one, Aragorn clinging to his back. Strider is on the other. They wheel across an open space, through running apes, and speed down a terrace.

MA-GOG steps out on to a rock ledge. He holds a staff in one hand, his cloak thrown back over his shoulder, magnificent in the eerie light. He stares down at the chaos. Drak swings across a ladder and lands at his side -

DRAK
What is it?

MA-GOG
(wild)
A sign - the hand of Man passes across the face of God! Lookl He points to a terrace below - Will leads the other two escapees along a road and on to the iron bridge. Drak and Ma-Gog stare at them. Darkness engulfs them.
Out of the blackness, an image -

CHRIST ON THE CROSS
It's a stained-glass window in a huge cathedral. A priest is at the altar conducting Mass for the repose of the dead. We pull back to reveal a tiny white coffin - just big enough for a baby. Next to it is another coffin.
And another - a row of them.

PRIEST
And even now as sorrow has no end, we find comfort in the words of the Lord
Jesus Christ. Did he not say unto Mark -"suffer the little children to come unto me, for they are the Kingdom of Heaven. Now and forever." Amen.
The congregation - sad-eyed relatives and weeping parents - fill the pews.

CONGREGATION
Amen.
Pall-bearers lift up the tiny coffins. The organ starts to play. A soloist

- a tenor -steps to the side of the altar. He starts to sing the Latin hymn
"Penis Angelicas". The haunting words of the hymn fill the cathedral. They carry over
to -

THE SPACE DOME is lit up by banks of lights that turn night into day. The clock
tower above the biology building shows the time2.00am. Even so, the area bustles with
activity.

INSIDE THE DOME
An illuminated chart dominates one wall - just like the strategy map in the
Pentagon's war room. Every research center is identified - next to it is its function and
a list of personnel. We see Princeton, Stanford, Texas
A&M, Los Alamos. Tentacles reach out to Oxford, the Pasteur Institute, the
University of Beijing...
Below the chart are nitrogen-cooled Cray super-computers. We track through teams of
men and women processing data, satellite dishes feeding a communications network, a
video conference taking place in a corner, technicians routing and re-routing phone calls
and faxes.
We come to a glass wall. On the other side is Diamond -

A SMALL OFFICE
Glass doors seal out the electronic hum. Diamond, staring through the glass, looks
exhausted. DeMaupassent sits on a couch. He's in his shirt-sleeves, dark rings under his
eyes. Next to him is Bob, the young neurologist. He wears jeans and a t-shirt. On the
front it says
"I'll sleep when I'm dead."
The coffee table is piled with files, journal extracts and computer print-outs. A video
projector beams a complex molecular structure on to a screen.
Diamond rubs her eyes, trying to wipe away the fatigue.

DIAMOND
I'm sorry Luc - say that again.

DEMAUPASSANT
DEMAUPASSANT (CONT'D)
(kindly)
My fault, Billie - I rattle on too much. The result is - we've fixed the time frame.
He hits the projector - the image of a fetus developing normally in the womb appears
on the screen... deMAUPASSANT
The fetus develops normally through the first trimester. Then it happens - about sixteen
weeks and two days, everything falls apart. The whole chemical structure goes out of
control -
He flashes up another image - a fetus that is already aging remarkably.
deMAUPASSANT
Once it starts, it's irreversible. If we're going to stop it, we've got to intercede here -
He points at the slide of the normally developing fetus.

BOB
(taking over)
There's a trigger - some major fucking switch gets turned. That's what I've been working on. It's definitely in the mDNA. There's a fragment of one chromosome I'm looking at
-
He flicks a switch on the video projector. A slide of a human gene, massively magnified, popl on to the screen.

BOB (CONT'D)
It's so different, I call it the alien. How it got there, exactly what it does - I haven't got the first idea.., no fucking idea at all.
Diamond looks at his grim face. He seems totally defeated.

DIAMOND
(quietly)
Is it that bad?
He stares at the floor. There's not even a hint of the former arrogance.

BOB
Someone's dropped us in the middle of the Louvre. We're blind men and they've told us to find the Mona Lisa. There's four miles of galleries end we've got five minutes to do it. That's how I feel -and that's when rm optimistic.
Diamond turns to deMaupassant.

DIAMOND
Luc?

DEMAUPASSANT
I'm sixty-two years old. I've seen us go from DC3s to landing on the moon.
In my life I've won all the glittering prizes. I've always believed nothing was beyond the reach of Man, but I'll tell you honestly - this may never be unraveled. If it is, it won't be in my lifetime.
He looks at them. Silence. There's nothing anyone can say. He starts to gather up his papers-

DEMAUPASSANT (CONT'D)
So what do we do? I think it's like Gatsby -"so we beat on, boats against the current, borne back ceaselessly into the past." There's no other way, ia there?
They nod their hoods - you have to try. DeMaupaasant and Bob start to leave.

DIAMOND
Luc?
(he turns))
You're certain - about the time, I mean?

DEMAUPASSANT
(Nodding)
Sixteen weeks. How far along are you?

DIAMOND
Twelve weeks.
They look at one another. The old man speaks gently -

DEMAUPASSANT
Good night, Billie.

A TINY FETUS perfectly formed - floats in the amniotic fluid. It's alive - the large head sways, the heart beats through the translucent ribs.
Diamond has her shirt pulled up and her jeans down around her thighs. She lies on a stainless steel table in a hi-tach examination room. A complex array of equipment - ultra-sounds and scanners - beams down on her exposed stomach. It projects a , video image onto a screen.
She is alone in the room, manipulating the equipment herself. She stares up at the child growing in her womb. We see the genitalia.

DIAMOND
So - you're a little boy. It's funny - I think I knew.
She reaches up and gently touches the image of his face.

DIAMOND (CONT'D)
We've got four weeks. The way I see it -there's nothing to lose. I can't tell you whet'll happen to us. It's on the edge, mister. The air's so thin out there, we may not even be able to breathe. But what the hell - it's a chance.
She takes her hand away and looks at his face.

DIAMOND (CONT'D)
You want to try it? Sure you do. You're my son. We've waited all our lives for each other.

A STACK OF HAND-WRITTEN NOTEPADS lie on a table in the basement. We track through them - past computer print-outs and dog-eared journals. We recognize them - these are Will's detailed notes.
To the table is the makeshift lab - racks of bottles and syringes. In the dim light we see Diamond. She removes the catheter from her vein, turns and climbs up the flotation tank.

INSIDE THE TANK
Water sloshes back and forth. Diamond lowers herself in and floats there.
For a moment, she stares up at the circle of light spilling through the hatch. We hold on her face.

DIAMOND (CONT'D)
(softly)
So we beat on, boats against the current.
She reaches up and pulls the hatch shut. Clang! Darkness.

THE SUN AND THE MOON
It's one of those strange twilights when both celestial bodies hang in the sky together.
Smoke drifts across them. We tilt down to ape city -
A column of smoke and flame spirals out of a stone chimney on top of the
slaughterhouse.

RED HOT FIRE burns in a huge furnace at one end of the slaughterhouse. The rickety
conveyor belt is working, clattering away. Several ape workers throw the bodies of the
lab animals - the dead tribes-people - on to the belt.
The body of the young boy is carried forward on the belt. It dumps him into the furnace.
The flames engulf him.

WILL'S EMPTY CELL
The door hangs open. The space is lit by a dozen torches. Drak is alone, moving around
the cell, trying to work out how Will escaped. He looks at the smashed bed, the hole in
the wall, the torn clothing that made the harness.
He swings the heavy door on its hinges and touches the lock. No answers there. Lying
in the doorway is the length of wood with the nail in the end.
Drak picks it up. He turns it over in his hand, th!nking about it.
He jumps! One handed he catches hold of the bars above the door.
Effortlessly, he hauls himself up and pokes the wood through the bars. The nail touches
the lock.

DRAK
(to himself)
Clever... you clever fucking animal.

DOCTOR ZORA (O.S.)
My lord...
He turns and sees the doctor hurrying towards him.

DOCTOR ZORA (CONT'D)
(urgent)
Could I see you please?

THE HALL OF POWER is a magnificent room - stone columns and towering trees
growing in huge pots. At one end is a rock shelf - open to the gathering twilight.
Silhouetted against it, commanding a view of the entire city, is the
Council of Elders. They sit around a table made from bone and tusks, deep in discussion.
Nazgul looks up - he sees Drak approaching through the shadows.

NAZGUL
Drak. I was just saying - maybe it's a blessing.

DRAK
A blessing?

NAZGUL
Where there's one, there must be others. If we'd killed him, we might never find them.

MA-GOG
But the animal's not stupid - he knows come day-break we'll be tracking him. Who's to say he'll run for home?
Drak stops in front of them.

DRAK
No - he's not stupid. But even dogs hunt in packs of seven. Every animal needs its kind. And when we find them - what then?

MA-GOG
What do you think?!

DRAK
Just like the tribes - burn them out of their holes, put them to the sword?
I don't mind doing that - I like it - but it's never enough, is it? No matter how many we kill, every year they're still here. Why will it be any different with the Blue Eyes? What we need is a final solution.
NAZGUL And where do we find that?

DRAK (CONT'D)
Doctor Zora's brought back patients from a place called Kismatu. I've been talking to her about it -
Several of the Council are looking at each other - perplexed.

MA-GOG
What is Kismatu?

NAZGUL
It's a tiny colony farther out than even the northern frontier. Females and babies have been dying there.
He turns to Drak - his eyes intense, very interested.

NAZGUL (CONT'D)
Go on.

COOL AND LOVELY ROOM

There are iron barn on I series of high windows but in the middle of the room is a jungle-gym. Underneath it are ape toys. Five baby apes sit on cots. They must be no more than two or three years old but their faces end bodies are those of old, old apeswizened and wrinkled, frail with age.

A double set of bars provide a sort of air-lock. Hanging on them is a sign "Quarantine. No Entry".

Drak and the Council of Elders stare in at the children. Doctor Zora is with them - she's nervous, twisting her fingers.

DOCTOR ZORA

We don't know what causes it- a virus probably. I'd hoped to complete our research before I came to you with my proposal. But, given the circumstances -

NAZGUL I

It's a brilliant idea.

(turns and smiles at her)

Brilliant.

HORSES' HOOVES paw the ground. They're bound with cloth to stop them leaving a trail. It's night -the horses are tethered near a fire burning in the lee of a rock.

Will and Strider have made camp - a hare roasts over the fire. Aragorn sits well apart - a silhouette in the moonlight - staring out into the forest, lost in his thoughts. Will and Strider look at him.

STRIDER

He's their leader - he can never take his eye from the mountain. He has to do what he thinks is right.

WILL

(hard)

By killing them?

STRIDER

Don't judge him, Will. I couldn't have done it. I wonder if you could? One of those women he just killed wes his daughter.

Will reacts. He turns and stares at the silhouette. A long beat.

WILL

(quietly)

We call it a Iobotomy. What other things have you people tried?

He turns to face him. Strider shrugs. There's something about it - something almost evasive.

WILL (CONT'D)

Fuck you, Strider! Tell me!

He stares at Will - he's never seen him angry.

STRIDER don't know if it's true.., my sister's mate works in the lab. He says
Doctor Zora's working on some disease -
Will comes towards him -

WILL
What sort of disease?

STRIDER
Of the children, I think - ape children.

WILL
How did they die, Strider? Old in the belly -is that how?!

STRIDER
Some of them. You know this disease?
Will stares at him, taking it in.

WILL
(softly)
So that's how it happened. Fuck you people.

STRIDER
They haven't done it yet. It may not work.

WILL
They will and it does.
He turns end takes step towards the forest. He runs his fingers through his hair -WILL
God help us.

STRIDER
That's funny - that's exactly what an ape would say.
Will turns. He and Strider stare at one another - the ape and the man, both struck by the
sudden commonality.

STRIDER (CONT'D)
I'm sorry...
Will walks slowly back to the fire. Strider starts to strip the meat off a hare he's roasting
over the flames. He offers it to Will. He shakes his head - he's not hungry anymore. He
stares into the flames -

WILL
What about you, Strider - why were you in the cell?

STRIDER

I fought another ape. Nothing very heroic, I'm afraid - I was drunk. He fell badly, his head hit the branch of a tree going down. It broke his neck.
He pauses We're not like humans. An ape never kills one of his own. Never.

WILL
What's the punishment?

STRIDER
At the ceremony of summer rites, the high priest would curse me with death.
I would have been left to die in the forest -no journey over the waterfall, no-one to say the sacred words. Without that, no ape can walk in the next world. You saved my life, Will and I'm grateful. But there's nothing I can do about my soul. I'm a dead ape walking.
Strider stripe more meet off the hare. Will picks up a saddle and blanket and starts to make himself bed.

STRIDER (CONT'D)
You knew, didn't you? You knew the sun was going to swallow the moon.
That's why you weren't afraid.
Will pauses - then he turns to him.

WILL
Yes - I knew.

STRIDER
WHO ARE YOU, WILL?
WILL
I've come a long way, Strider - it's farther then I can explain.

STRIDER
I've heard stories - old apes tell them 'round the fire late at night - of strange lands where the creatures can tell the future. Is that where you're from?

WILL
In a way.. yeah, it's something like that.

STRIDER
So what happens to it afl, to the world we've built? Tell me that.

WILL
It passes away.
Strider stares at him through the firelight.

STRIDER
History remembers, though - it's passed on, what we did, I mean?

WILL
No, Strider - there's nothing, not a trace left behind.
Strider thinks for a moment, then he smiles gently.

STRIDER
So it's just vanity then - what we believe, that the works of the ape will last forever?

WILL
Yes, it's vanity. But not just of apes, Strider -maybe of men, too.
He turns and settles down on his makeshift bed. Strider - the food forgotten - stares out into the night. A million stars hang on a velvet sky.
Look down from them - in the vast blackness of the forest, one tiny lightthe flickering fire.

DUST SWIRLING, HOOVES POUNDING battalions of ape cavalry sweep out of the stables. Dawn is breaking across the city. Ma-Gog stands on a ridge, his staff raised, blessing the army as it rides out.
At its head is Drak. He clatters across the iron and wood bridge and down the avenue of idols. Votive fires burn in front of every statue.

A RAINBOW arches across the end of a tiny gorge. Dozens of streams cascade into pools, spilling over ledges and swirling into ponds. Aragorn leads Will and
Strider along a hidden, path - a rock ledge that runs behind the waterfalls.
The ledge widens into a large cave. Sunlight streams through a veil of cascading water.
Aragorn looks around - something's worrying him.

ARAGORN
This is the Rainbow Tribe's cave. They should be here.

A STONE FIREPLACE
Aragorn places his hand on the circle of stones, feeling its warmth.

ARAGORN (CONT'D)
They left at the rising of the sun.
He moves deeper into the cave - a maze of limestone caverns and passage-ways. He stops at sleeping area - weapons lie there, food in baskets.

ARAGORN
(softly)
Why such hurry?
Suddenly he stops, listening. He looks at Strider -

ARAGORN (CONT'D)
You heard it?
Strider nods his head - yes. Will hasn't heard a thing. He listens hard - nothing.

ARAGORN (CONT'D)
Animal?

STRIDER
I don't think so.
Strider moves silently to the side of the cave. He picks up a crossbow.

STRIDER (CONT'D)
Is there another entrance?

ARAGORN
From the ridge above. Apes?

STRIDER
Scouts probably.
He cocks the crossbow. Aragorn has picks up a bow and spear. He moves towards a cavern, signaling Strider to take a passageway.
Will grabs a crossbow. Strider tosses him a chain mail vest - armor. They move off.

HONEYCOMB OF PASSAGES eep in the cave. A sound - pebbles falling off a ledge. Then we see a flicker of light - a torch is moving through a cavern. Whoever holds it, turns a corner and is lost in darkness.

A CROSSROADS of arches and stalactites. Will and Strider split apart. Will moves silently through the darkness, into a cavern. Through an archway he sees a shadow on the wall! He goes fast towards it -

A HUGE BOULDER
The shadow comes round the boulder. We tilt down and now we see who's holding the torchDiamondl She's armed with a crossbow - cocked end loaded.
She turns a corner -
Ten feet in front of her is Strider. She stares at the massive ape's back - a bandoleer of arrows slung over his shoulder. Her eyes widen with fear.
She raises the crossbow -
Strider hears it. He spins, weapon rising - turns into a passage midway between them.
He sees Diamond about to fire. He screams -
Too late - she pulls the trigger! Will hurls himself forward - in front of
Strider. Whack! The arrow blasts into his chest. He crashes to the ground.
Diamond stares down at him.

DIAMOND
Will!
His eyes open - he's gasping for breath from the impact. He and Diamond look at one another. Strider reaches down and rips the arrow out of Will's chain mail armor. Diamond's shoulders sag with relief.

DIAMOND (CONT'D)
(indicates Strider Who's he?

WILL
I'll explain later.
He struggles to his feet and looks at Diamond -

WILL (CONT'D)
What made you come? I thought the mDNA was just a theory. One of dozens of theories
- isn't that what you said?

DIAMOND
We did a lot of work. I guess I was wrong.

WILL
People have been wrong about a lot of things.

THE GREAT VALLEY stretches out below - primordial forests and cascading streams. Will and
Diamond stand on a rock ledge outside the cave.

WILL (CONT'D)
This is the rift valley in Kenya -
He points at the towering, snow-capped peak.

WILL (CONT'D)
That's Kilamanjaro - ten thousand feet higher but a hundred thousand years of wind and rain will turn it into the mountain we know. Think of it - we've come back a hundred thousand years! Everyone told me it couldn't be done, but we've crossed the frontier now - Man has traveled through space and time. How long has science dreamed of that?

DIAMOND
How long have you?

WILL
All my life.

DIAMOND
Dream no more. You've done it. Like you said in your note - it was Doctor
Robert Plant of UC Berkeley.
WILL turns and looks out at the valley -

WILL
(softly)
Yeah - I really have, haven't I?
Diamond watches him. There's a shout from inside the cave -

STRIDER (O.S.)
Aragorn - I've found it!

A CAVE PAINTING
Newly-drawn, is hidden in e nook high up in the main cave. Strider, Will and Diamond
watch aa Aregorn looks at it by torchlight.

ARAGORN
I thought they would leave word for their hunters. Kip-Kena has called a gathering of
the Seven Tribes.

WILL
Where?

ARAGORN
Two days' travel - at the Eagle's Nest.
He looks out through the mouth of the cave - twilight is closing in.

ARAGORN (CONT'D)
We'll stay hera tonight. Be ready to leave at first light.

THE EMBERS OF A FIRE burn in the circle of stoncs. Aragorn and Strider are
sleeping next to it.
Will and Diamond have been awake all night. They sit in the shadows near the entrance
to the cave, speaking quietly.

DIAMOND
An ape civilization? You said there was a city.., what happened to it all?

WILL
You know what we've found of Aragorn's whole race? Seventeen bones, that's all.
Anthropologists have discovered evidence of the apes - we call them skulls. Bones last
a lot longer than civilizations.

DIAMOND
I guess there's a lesson in that.

WILL
Listen, Billie - the apes have discovered a disease.
Diamond reacts. Will crouches down - in the dirt he scratches out a small chain of
circles. It's a molecule.

WILL (CONT'D)
It's really rare and, lucky for them, it's in an isolated area. They're not stupid - they
understand it's potential. They plan to give it to the tribes

He draws an arrow from the molecule to a bow-legged stick figure of a man.

WILL (CONT'D)
And maybe they do, but it doesn't matter -Aragorn's people aren't us.
Already evolution's taken another track - scratches a cross through the bow-legged man.
He draws the figure of an upright human.

WILL (CONT'D)
Somewhere in the rift valley is someone like us - the first man.

DIAMOND
Woman. You said it was in the mitochondrial DNA - it has to be a woman.
She reaches forward and scratches long hair on to the figure's head.

WILL
You're right. Sooner or later the apes find her. She doesn't look like the tribes but the apes don't care - she's human.
So they give her the disease. She's different though - it doesn't work, or at least it doesn't seem to. It gets integrated into her. It's passed on, it mutates, it weaves its way into the mDNA. It lies there - a bomb waiting to go off. And then one day -

DIAMOND
After a hundred thousand years?

WILL
The planet's five billion years old. What's that to Nature? A blink of the eye.
Will throws the stick down on the ground.

WILL (CONT'D)
That's the theory, anyway.

DIAMOND
(impressed)
A helluva theory, Doctor Plant.

HE TURNS AND LOOKS IT HER -
DIAMOND (CONT'D)
There's not much time, Will. We have to find her before the apes and we have to do it within four weeks.

WILL
Jesus, Billie! Four weeks? We've got a theory - that's all. We don't even know half the problems we're dealing with. You can't put a deadline on science.

DIAMOND
Science, Will? What about people? Isn't that what this is all about. I'm sorry - I thought there were children dying.

WILL
Sure. Of course it's about that too.

DIAMOND
But then, you don't care muchabout people do you?

THEY LOOK AT ONE ANOTHER. A BEAT. WILL'S VOICE IS HARD -
WILL
No - I guess I don't. Not for a long time. Ideas and knowledge are what matter. They're the shining ideals. That's the only way we progress.

DIAMOND
Progress to what? We're both children of our age, aren't we? We've grown up to believe the more we know, the more advanced we are. But what does that mean if we've forgotten the things of real value. You know the reason I came? It's got nothing to do with science or knowledge. I'm going to have a child -that's why I'm here.
They look at one another.

DIAMOND (CONT'D)
Uke you said, the women's out there somewhere. Why ere we traveling with them? (indicates Aragore and Strider)
We should cut ourselves loose.

WILL
We wouldn't last a day. We've got to keep moving, Billie. The apes are like storm-troopers.

DIAMOND
Where are they now?

WILL
Right behind. I think Strider has some sort of tribal intuition. He says he can hear their hoof beats in his head.
The first rays of dawn pierce the mist from the waterfall. Will and Diamond turn at a sound behind them - Aragorn is getting up.

ARAGORN
Ready?

A SPARKLING RIVER winds through a beautiful valley. The two horses splash along the water's edge. Strider and Aragorn are mounted on one, Will and Diamond on the other. They turn a curve - Aragorn leads them out of the shallows and into the forest.

THE CAVE OF THE RAINBOW
Ape soldiers are swarming over the cave. A TRACKER uses torchlight to study footprints. He looks up at Orak -

TRACKER
There's four of them, my Lord.

DRAK
Four? The Tracker points It a at of prints -

TRACKER
It's woman. Blue Eyes has a mate.

DRAK
Excellent. I look forward to meeting her.

SOLDIER (O.S.)
My Lord - hoof prints.
Drak turns - the man stands on a path that curves up towards the roof of the cave. Drak looks up - high above he sees a slash of daylight. It's another entrance.

DRAK
Malakai! Bolag!
Two heavily-armed officers emerge from among the soldiers. With Drak they run for the wall. They leap up the rock face - their massive hands grabbing tiny ledges.
Other apes follow them. They scramble up the wall with amazing speed.

AN EAGLE CIRCLES
Soaring and hovering in the sky. We tilt down a tribesman - dressed in skins edged with feathers - is perched high on a jagged peak. He's a
LOOKOUT. He tenses -
Four figures on foot appear on a path cut into the side of a cliff. The Lookout gives a piercing crythe sound of an eagle. It carries down to -

SERIES OF WOODEN PLATFORMS are built into the rocky crags, opening into caves. They are connected by ladders and bridges slung across dizzying drops. The inhabitants here live with their totem -this is the nest of the Tribe of the Eagle.
The platforms and caves are crowded with the gathering tribes. People turn at the Lookout's cry. A man pushes through, listening - it's Kip-Kena.

THE LOOKOUT POST
Kip follows the direction of the Lookout's pointing finger. Will and
Diamond lead the other two - all on foot now - along the path.

KIP

It's the traveler! With a woman...
The Lookout shields his eyes against the sun - the visitors ere coming closer.

LOOKOUT
The fool - he's brought an ape with himl He reaches for a bow but Kip's hand falls on
his arm, stopping him.

KIP
Who's the other one, though?
(realizing)
Aragorn!
He turns, yelling down to the platforms -

KIP (CONT'D)
It's the Ranger! The Ranger is free!

ON THE PLATFORMS
The tribes-people burst into action - running for the bridges, scaling the ladders.

A WOODEN BRIDGE SWINGS THROUGH THE AIR
Whack! It locks into place on the far side of a deep crevasse. It's a primitive drawbridge.
Aragorn steps on to it, leading the others across.
The tribes-people are gathering, eager to greet him. Then thcy see Strider.
A ripple of fear and anger runs through them.

ARAGORN
The ape travels with me - treat him as a friend.
Nobody argues with the Ranger. He stops in front of Kip. The young warrior starts to
bow his head but Aragorn stops him. He puts out his arms - they embrace.
Will crosses the bridge. Kip sees him. He grasps Will's arm in greeting -

KIP
You carry part of my spirit with you -I owe you my life. Welcome, Traveler.

INSIDE THE EAGLE'S NEST
A series of caves, connected by vaulted arches, extend in to the mountain.
They're crowded with members of various tribes - children are playing, flint-knappers
are fashioning tools, women ara cooking.
A shaft of sunlight strikes a ledge high up the wall. Kip and Will have found a quiet
place amid the bustle.

WILL
Are the seven tribes here?

KIP

All except the Antelope. They hunt the plains far to the west - they have the longest journey.

WILL
Will they come?

KIP
Who knows - maybe the apes have found them. Nobody has seen them for many summers gone. Why?

WILL
I'm searching for someone - a young woman. She looks like us ...
(he indicates Diamond))
I thought she might live with the tribes.

KIP
Is she a relative - was she born to your hearth?

WILL
To all of our hearths. My race reveres her. We think of her as the first woman. Without her. our lives are nothing.

KIP
(nodding his head)
Women are of the spirit - we believe that. too. Mother Earth mates with the totems. Only through woman can their children walk the world.

WILL
Have you seen her?

KIP
NO.
WILL
You're sure? Perhaps some of the women have seen something?

KIP
She looks like you, you say? No offense, Traveler, but the women say you're the ugliest man they've ever seen. A woman that looks like you - I'm sure they would have talked about it.

WILL
Ugly?
They smile at one another.

KIP
I'm sorry I can't help.

A torch flares below. Kip looks down into an adjoining cave. It's empty except for a group of men - all warriors - filing in. These are the leaders of each of the tribes.

ANOTHER TORCH IS LIT
They ring the walls of the small cave. By their light we see the skins, the feathers and the symbols of each tribe's totem - the eagle, the tiger, the rainbow...
Beneath each one squats its leader. One place is empty - the Tribe of the Antelope. Will sits near the entrance. He watches Aragorn - dressed in ceremonial robes, the Crescent of Light glistening at his neck - rise to his feet.

ARAGORN
We've traveled without rest - there are soldiers a day behind. The ape says it's an army.

KIP
And there are more coming from the north. Five squadrons et least, the runners say. It's led by the old warrior Nazgul.

ARAGORN
Is that why you called the gathering?

KIP
Great things are moving, Ranger -
An old man, battle-scarred and gray, leans forward. He is thc leader of the Rainbow.

A RAINBOW
A stranger walks out of the west, the moon hides the sun, armies are on the march - come the new moon, nothing in Middle Earth will be the same.
Others nod their heads in agreement.

KIP (CONT'D)
We either fight or flee - the Tribes must decide.

ARAGORN
I know you, Kip - you always were a fighter. What do the others say? warrior in a feathered cloak speaks -

EAGLE
It doesn't matter what we say - the Ranger has returned. We'll follow wherever he leads.
Aragorn looks at their faces. Slowly he shakes his head -

ARAGORN
I'll walk the path Mother Earth has laid for me, but I'll walk it no more as Ranger.
The leaders stare at him. Several start to object but he silences them with his hand -

ARAGORN

A man leads from his heart and winter has come early to mine.
(softly)
I took the life of my daughter - and some of your kinfolk with it. I did my duty -nothing
more can be asked of I men. But now others must walk in my place.
He walks forward, unfastening the Crescent of Light. He stops in front of
Kip -

ARAGORN
If I should have had a son, I would have hoped for a man as fine as you.
This is my last act as Ranger of the Easterlings-
He reaches out and slips the Crescent of Light around Kip's neck.

ARAGORN (CONT'D)
Take care of my father's people. Guide them well.
(he looks at the leaders)
You must decide what is best for the Tribes. For me... I was the one that had to strike
the blow, but it was the apes who killed my child. Tomorrow I will go to fight them.
What father could do any less?
He turns away and walks towards the entrance. Only Will sees the tears in his eyes.

KIDS' FACES, WIDE-EYED
They huddle together - staring at the strange-looking woman and the ape.
Strider is building a small fire at the side of the cave, Diamond lays down furs for
sleeping. , She looks up - the leaders are coming out of the meeting. Will approaches.

WILL
They're going to war. They leave at dawn.

STRIDER
They'll be slaughtered.

WILL
They think if they leave the valley, their totems won't follow. Without them, they say
they're dead anyway.

DIAMOND
We should go now.
Will looks at her. She meets his gaze. Suddenly she realizes -

DIAMOND
Oh, nol We're not fighting someone else's war -

WILL
Listen to me -

DIAMOND

We've got four weeks, Willl Four weeks to find her. She's not here, so whet are we waiting for? Let's go!
The tribes-people turn at the raised voices. Will takes Diamond's arm and guides her to a private corner -

WILL
Listen, Billie! We know the future - but if we beat the apes, they can't harm the woman.

DIAMOND
Beat the apes?! And say we don't - or say one of us gets captured. What then? Don't you understand? Four weeksi

WILL
Yeah, I understand - but those things aren't going to happen. We know things the apes can't even dream of. This is our world, Billie - men won it with their minds. All we need is knowledge and science. We've got them both. We can win!

DIAMOND
What are we going to do - dazzle them with calculus? This is an army, Will
- you said it yourself. Storm-trooperst

WILL
Look -
He bends and picks up s rock from the ground. He hands it to Diamond -

WILL (CONT'D)
Taste it. That's saltpeter - the natural form of potassium nitrate. The caves are littered with the stuff. You've smelt the air - there's sulfur all around. If we burn timber, that'll give us charcoal. You're s scientist
- you know what it means.
Sure - she knows what it means. She stares at him.

DIAMOND
It's strange, isn't it? Give s man s problem and the first thing he thinks about is weapons.

WILL
We're a frail species, Billea. It's only weapons that have made us bigger than we are.

DIAMOND
Or smaller.

WILL
It's the apes who are going to be a whole lot smaller after this. We can beat themi No more experiments - no more problem.

DIAMOND

(quietly)
I hope your right, Will.

FIRES BURN all over the eagle's nest, turning piles of timber into charcoal. The camp is a hive of activitycolumns of tribes-people make their way up from the valley carrying piles of sulfur rock; women and children sit in circles, pounding the saltpeter into dust. Will moves among the tribal leaders, watching as they measure and combine the elements in bowls.
Strider sits apart, watching, not sure if the humans have lost their minds.

STRAW MAN FLIES TOWARDS US
He looks like a scarecrow except he's dressed in captured ape armor. Rigged to a flying fox, he speeds past a rock face. All of the tribes-people are gathered on the side of a crevasse, watching.
The straw men flies closer - towards a rocky outcrop. Will touches a burning ember to the ground. We see a flash of flame as a fuse ignites but we lose it among the rocks. A thin trail of smoke marks its passage.
The tribes-people watch - nothing seems to be happening. Suddenly - just as the straw man reaches the outcrop -
Ka-boom! A huge explosion. Fire and flying rock hit the straw men.
The tribes-people scream. Terrified, they turn and run. Smoke and dust obscure the flying fox. Will walks forward to examine his handiwork.
Tribes-people peer out from their hiding places - the smoke and dust clear.
They see the tattered shreds of the straw man hanging from the rope.
Several of the women start to cry in fear.
Will stands on the edge of the crevasse. He turns - Kip, Aragorn and the other leaders are approaching. They look at him with trepidation.

KIP
You make fire from rocks of the earth -what is this thing?

WILL
Gunpowder.
Kip turns to the others. They repeat the word, as if that will unlock its mystery.

WILL (CONT'D)
We've still got work to do.
He turns and goes. The tribes-people, emboldened by their leaders, come closer. They draw back from Will as he makes his way through them. He comes face to face with Strider. The man and the ape look at one another.

STRIDER
Apes believe men are the devil's children. Maybe they're right. What have you done, Will - what have you unleashed on the world?

WILL

Nothing, Strider. The future, that's all.

STRIDER
I can't fight with you tomorrow, Will. To kill an ape in a brawl is one thing, but I can't go to war against my people.

WILL
(kindly)
I never expected you to.
Again they look at one another. Will turns and leaves.

WATER FLYING, HOOVES POUNDING
Drak and his cavalry, pennants flying, gallop along the edge of a river.
Ranks of infantry, followed by horse-drawn supply wagons, travel behind.
The river swings around a point thick with trees. We crane up above the foliage - a tributary flows clown the other side. Marching through the shallows is another army of apes. At their head, on a stallion, is Nazgul.
The two squadrons converge at the end of the point. The foot soldiers meld together, the Praetorian Guard splash ahead, Drak and Nazgul ride side by side. Ahead, the river and its tributary pour over a broad rock ledge. It's a natural weir -

THE FORD OF THE THREE RIVERS
A jumble of logs and broken branches lie snagged in the middle of the river. The Praetorian Guard sweep past them and turn on to the weir.
The Guard spur their horses forward, forcing them through the fast-running current, crossing to the other side -

IN THE TREES
A shadow of movement. Tribesmen glide through the dappled light of the forest, almost invisible in skins and camouflage.
Will and Kip stand motionless, deep in shadow. They watch as the Guard on their horses come thundering across the ford, straight towards them. The infantry are close behind. Will drops his hand -

TRAILS OF FIRE whip along the ground - out of the forest and on to the flattened rocks that form part of the ford. The Guards' horses shy away. The apes look down in puzzlement -
Boom! Boom! Booml Sections of the weir explode in plumes of rock and water.
Apes are cut to pieces, horses are hurled into the fast-flowing water.
On the far side - Orak's horse rears up. He drives his spurs into its flanks, trying to control it. Clouds of dust and smoke billow across the weir, the wounded are screaming - the ape cavalry wheel and turn in confusion.
Drak plunges forward - chaos all around him. He pounds his chest with both fists and roars -

DRAK

Apes - chargel
The apes still on their horses hear his cry. They spur their mounts forward. The first of
the cavalry reach -

THE SHORE
Boom... boom! More explosions rip the river bank to pieces.

IN THE FOREST
Batteries of cross-bows are mounted on a series of long wooden frames. The
Eagle leader and his warriors run from one to the other, touching flames to rope fuses.
Fire sizzles towards the crossbows, each one loaded with a charge -
Bam...bam...bamf The scores of crossbows fire.

ON THE FORD
The ape cavalry are plunging through the smoke and debris. Wham! The hail of arrows
cut them to pieces.
Drak is in the middle of a whirling mass of apes and horses. He looks through the smoke
- into the forest. He sees Will, standing on a rock with
Kip, like a general commanding his army.
Drak bellows with rage. He snaps the reins, about to drive his horse onward. An arrow
flies in from the flank. Whackt It slams into Drak's chest armor, splintering. He turns -

THE JUMBLE OF LOGS floats in the middle of the river. The leader of the Rainbow
Tribe, water streaming off of him, kneels on the tangle of trees and branches, reloading
his bow. This is no jumble of logs - it's a firing platform they've anchored therel dozen
Rainbow warriors, hidden in the water, clamber out of the river. They kneel next to their
leader, drlwing their bows -

THE FORD
Drak watches es I flight of arrows slam into the milling ranks of apes.
Right in front of him, an arrow rips through the throat of the leader of the Praetorian
Guard. Drak turns to Nazgul, yelling -

DRAK
The ones in the river - take themi Nazgul spurs his horse back across the weir.

ON THE SHORE
Ape cavalry and infantry scramble up the river bank. Bam! They hear the charges go
off - the hurl themselves down. Another volley of arrows scythes through them -

IN THE FOREST
The Eagle leader and his men work feverishly to reload and recharge the batteries of
crossbows. One of the warriors looks up - terror on his face.
Drak, followed by the remnants of his Praetorian Guard, charge through the blue haze
of gunsmoke - straight towards them.

One of the crossbow batteries fires! Arrows hit his horse's armor but Drak doesn't falter. Crouched Iow in the saddle, he spins the Gatling gun like a gunslinger. He locks it under his arm.

The eagle warriors start to break and run. The apes' horses sound like thunder rolling closer. The Eagle leader and several of his warriors stand their ground, desperately working to reload.

They spin the battery, sighting straight at Drak's chest. They fire! Arrows fly -

Drak leaps out of the saddle! He catches hold of an overhanging bough. The arrows whiz underneath, skimming his butt. He leaps again - higher into the tree.

The Eagle leader looks up - sunlight sparkles on the leaves. It's dazzling

-

Smash! Drak's sword cleaves through one of the warriors. Drak has dropped to the ground, right behind them. The Eagle leader turns - too latel

Rat-a-tat-tat! The Gatling gun fires. Arrows shred the Eagle leader's feathered coat. He crumples to the ground like some fallen bird.

THE FORD

The ape infantry pour across the ford, charging over the bodies of their fallen comrades.

THE FOREST

Riderless horses, part of the ape cavalry, charge wildly through the trees.

We tilt up - their riders have abandoned them and taken to the trees. The branches are thick with apes firing, cutting down groups of running tribesmen.

THE ROCK PLATFORM

Will and several tribesmen hurl camouflage aside revealing a long iron barrel wedged in the rocks. One of the warriors tilts it up, aiming it at the trees; another stokes pebbles and scraps of metal into the barrel.

Will touches an ember to a fuse. Everyone dives for cover -

Boom! The primitive cannon fires. The shrapnel hits the trees. Shredded apes, branches and leaves fall to the ground.

Will and the warriors reload. Again they fire - but the charge is too big.

The whole cannon breaks free of the rocks. It flies like a missile and smashes into the trunk of a tree. Timber!

A ROCKY GORGE

Its rugged walls are lined with piles of huge boulders. Aragorn and a group of warriors are fighting hand-to-hand, being forced back by scores of ape infantry.

Aragorn drives his spear at a huge ape. The point plunges into the animal's belly, up and under his armor. Blood spurts out from the joins in the metal.

IN THE TREES

An ape sharpshooter sights down his crossbow - straight at Aragorn. He fires -

AMONG THE BOULDERS

Wham! The crossbow bolt smashes into Aragorn's shoulder, sending him reeling. One of the tribesmen turns - it's Kip. He sees Aragorn on his knees.
Kip wields a sword, fighting his way towards Aragorn. Slash! He takes one ape across the chest. Whaml Another ape in the neck. He grabs Aragorn and starts to drag him out of the melee.

IN THE TREES

The ape sharpshooter has Kip in his sights. His finger reaches for the trigger. He starts to squeeze -
Sswhishl The sound of an arrow. Whackl It buries itself in the sharpshooter's neck. He falls out of the tree -

HIGH AMONG THE BOULDERS

Will. He stands almost at the top of the gorge, lowering a crossbow. He looks down at Kip's men - the apes, vastly superior in numbers, are swarming forward, driving the tribesmen back.
On a ridge below him, four tribesmen scramble away from huge boulder. A flash of fire then - Ka-bam!

ON THEGROUND

Apes are rushing forward. They hear the explosion. Several apes turn - the huge boulder, split into chunks, flies towards them. The apes scatter.
Smashl The chunks knock apes aside like skittles.
But there's more of them behind, spilling in to the gorge, over-running it

-

THE DUST FROM THE EXPLOSION swirls past Drak. He looks up - he sees Will on the ridge, silhouetted against the sky.
Drak snarls deep in his throat. He wheels his horse and gallops hard towards a trail that winds up among the boulders.

ON THE RIDGE

Will moves fast along the top of the ridge. He stops - looking down on the river. On the other side, Nazgul and a platoon of apes unload huge leather bladders from the wagons and empty them into the river.
Will shades hil ayes - the water glistens with iridescent colors. He realizes - it's oil.
The current carries it straight towards the platform in the river. The warriors of the Rainbow tribe - unaware - are still aboard, firing at the apes on the ford.
Will turns fait - wa whip pan along the shoreline. He sees what he feared - two apes below him with a fire burning. They slot flaming arrows into their crossbows -
Will unslings his crossbow, steadies himself and fires -
Ks-whack! The arrow rips through one ape's neck. He pitches forward - heed-first into the fire. The other ape hurls himself aside, diving for cover.
Will re-loads. The side of the ape's head is just visible behind a rock. If Will makes this, it's going to be a helluva shot.

His finger curls around the trigger - right behind him, the sound of hooves. Will spins it's Drak charging towards him. He raises the Gatling gun -
Will aims at the big ape's throat and fires.
Drak swerves. The arrow misses his throat but slams into his exposed forearm. The Gatling gun flies from his hand.
There's no time for Will to re-load - he turns and runs.
Drak charges down on him. He draws a harpoon out of its scabbard.
Will scrambles over a crest - nothing but thin air!
Drak has him square in his sights. He draws back his arm, about to hurl the harpoon. Will throws himself forward -

THE SIDE OF A CLIFF
Will falls down, down, down.
Drak reins his horse to a halt right at the edge. He looks over - Will plunges towards the river, flowing fast below the ford.
Splash! Will cannonballs into the water and disappears. Drak stares down, trying to catch sight of him. Nothing.

IN THE RIVER
A tree branch and other flotsam is being carried downstream by the current.
A pair of hands emerge from the water and grab hold of it. Will's head follows.
Gasping, catching his breath, he looks upstream - the water pours over the weir. A flaming arrow arcs through the air. The ape on the shore has done his job -

THE OIL SLICK erupts in flames as the arrow hits it. The whole surface of the river is suddenly transformed into a raging blaze.
The Rainbow leader and his men turn. They see a wall of flame racing towards them. Several warriors dive into the water, swimming for the shore

-
Whoosh! The flames engulf them. A wall of fire sweeps over the wooden platform. Like macabre shadows - we see the dancing shapes of the dying warriors.

IN THE RIVER
The current pulls Will down the river. He looks back - the molten fire spills over the weir. Anguished screams are carried on the wind. A pillar of black, oily smoke rises up high into the sky -

THE EAGLES' NEST
The platforms and rocky outcrops are crowded with the women, children and old folks. Diamond and Strider stand together. All of them stare down at the river valley. The pillar of smoke rises higher.

WOMAN (O.S.)
They're here!

Diamond turns - the woman is standing on the highest platform. Diamond follows the direction of her outstretched arm.
A group of warriors, followed by their women-folk and children, are coming round the mountain path. Their leader wears a golden fur and a head-dress of auroch's horns. It's the Tribe of the Antelope.

OUTSIDE THE MAIN CAVE
A chorus of chattering voices. The new arrivals are surrounded by members of their sister tribes. The leader of the Antelope stands in the center, listening to a woman -Kip's wife. Whatever she's saying is lost in the hubbub.

ANTELOPE
Quiet!
Instantly, the voices die.

ANTELOPE (CONT'D)
(anxious)
Where?
Kip's wife doesn't answer - she walks forward and points to the pillar of smoke. The Antelope leader turns to his warriors.

ANTELOPE (CONT'D)
We go - now!

DIAMOND AND STRIDER stand on the platform, watching several old men lower the drawbridge.
Whack! It locks into place. The antelope warriors cross it and disappear down a narrow trail.
The rest of the Antelope tribe move towards the cave. Diamond turns away - then she stops. Something has caught her eye. She stares at the crowd of women and children heading into the cave.

STRIDER
What is it?
Diamond doesn't answer - she tenses. In the milling crowd of brown bodies, she sees it again - a flash of gold. It*s sunlight on blonde hair.

DIAMOND
She's here.., holy God - she's herel It's not a woman - it's a child!
She grabs a rope ladder, ignores the rungs and slithers down it.

A YOUNG GIRL helps her mother set up camp. She is about 10 years old, tawny-haired, taller and straighter-backed'than any of her people. She looks like us.
Diamond pushes through the women and kids gathered around the hearth. She stops. The young girl turns. For a moment she and Diamond stare at one another, separated by a hundred thousand years, but so similar they can both see themselves in the other.

THE YOUNG GIRL SMILES. DIAMOND RETURNS IT -
DIAMOND
What's your name?
The girl's mother stares, amazed to see someone who looks like her child.

MOTHER
Her name is Aiv.

DIAMOND
Ev?
(Realizing)
Of course. My people have a name like that - "Eve" is how we say it.
The mother nods - the sound seems to please her. Diamond puts out her arms and indicates the young girl. The mother smiles, giving her permission.
Diamond puts her arms around Eve.

DIAMOND (CONT'D)
(softly)
I've come a long way to find you.
Eve looks at her - wide-eyed, innocent.

EVE
Why?

DIAMOND
To keep you safe.
She holds her tight. The mother catches Diamond's eye.

MOTHER
Do you have children?
Diamond shakes her head - no. The mother can't hide her disappointment.

DIAMOND
What's wrong?

MOTHER
I was hoping you had a son. Aiv's a sweet girl. She's the child of my heart. But the way she looks, nobody will want her as a mate.
Before Diamond can answer there's a commotion outside the cave. She turns to look - Strider and tribes-people are running out into the daylight.

SWIRLS OF DUST rise up from I mountain path. Whatever's causing it is hidden from view by the peaks and crags. The tribal-people gather on vantage points, watching it come closer. Strider cocks his head - listening. A shadow of fear passes across his face.

STRIDER
Horses! It's horses!

Horses mean apesi Panic sweeps through the tribes-people. Women grab their children, young kids start screaming, old men and boys scramble for weapons.

Diamond weaves through the flying mass of people. She swings up on to a platform beside Strider. He points -

Coming into view on the mountain path - running and stumbling, dragging their wounded - are what's left of the Antelope warriors.

Their women-folk cry out as they realize what has happened to their mates.

The warriors race along the path and across the drawbridge. Nobody raised it when they left -

Several old men and a couple of boys struggle now to do it. They haul on the ropes and pulleys. It starts to swing upwards -

Here he comes - Drak! He's galloping hard at the head of his cavalry, battle scarred and bloodied. He sees the drawbridge starting to lift. He doesn't pause - he whips his horse into a thundering gallop.

The bridge rises higher. Drak's horse leaps! It soars across the crevasse - the giddylng drop stretches out below - and lands on the lifting bridge.

The men and boys stare in horror. Orak charges down on them. They back away

-all except one boy, not even in his teens, who stands his ground.

Swish! Drak's sword cleaves him from shoulder to waist. The other tribesmen run. Wham! The drawbridge falls back into place. The ape cavalry charge across it.

BROAD WOODEN PLATFORM
An ape horseman flies across the platform. He leaps off the edge, on to a lower platform. Diamond's right in front of him!

She throws herself aside, grabs hold of a rope ladder and drops onto -

A ROCK SHELF
She looks across the broad area in front of the cave - apes everywhere, weapons flashing, people screaming.

A young boy tries to out-run an ape warrior - it's Gray Beard. The young boy hasn't got a chance. Gray Beard lashes out at him with a stock-whip.

It curls around the boy's ankle, tripping him. The boy looks up - he tries to shield his face. Too late! The horse's hooves smash down -

Diamond looks away, unable to watch. She sees Eve. The young girl is at the front of the cave, spinning in panic. Her mother runs towards her...

The mother doesn't see Gray Beard galloping towards her. Diamond screams a warning but it's just one more crv in the commotion.

Gray Beard raises a short-handled lance and hurls it like a javelin. It hits the mother in the small of the back, straight through the spine. She pitches forward - dead. Eve screams and runs towards her mother.

Diamond leaps off the rock ledge -

IN FRONT OF THE CAVE

Diamond runs faster than she's ever run, sprinting to grab Eva. Drak wheels his horse - he sees Diamond. His lip curls back and he smiles - one of the
Blue Eyes! And a woman! He leaps his horse forward -

DRAK
Grab the female!
Gray Beard is off his horse. Diamond runs towards him. He raises a crossbow...
Drak charges down on her from behind. He holds the harpoon at his shoulder.
He aims at her legs.
Diamond races on - her only thought, to save Eve. It'll never happen - she's as good as deadGray Beard's in front, aiming. Drak's right behind. He hurls the harpoon.
Whoosh! Strider swings through the air. He clings to one of the rope ladders - it's like Tarzan, except he's an ape. He grabs Diamond by the scruff of the neck and yanks her out of the way.
Drak's harpoon skims past them. Gray Beard stares in amazement at the woman flying through the air. But that's not his big surprise - with Diamond out of the way, the harpoon is flying straight at him. He screams as it rips into his throat.

HIGH ROCK LEDGE
Strider - Diamond clutched under his arm - lands on a ledge high above the fight. Diamond turns fast and looks back -

IN FRONT OF THE CAVE
Eve crouches over the body of her mother. The woman's mouth is frozen in an anguished scream, her dead eyes stare straight ahead. Eva shakes her, desperately hoping for some sign of life. Nothing. Eve starts to cry.
A dark shadow falls across her. She looks up - it's Drak. He reaches down and grabs her by the neck. He beats his chest with his fist and raises her up above his head like a trophy.

ON THE ROCK LEDGE
Diamond, anguished, tries to go to the little girl but Strider holds her in an iron grip. He swings Diamond off her feet, and leaps for an overhanging branch of a tree. He jumpsfrom the tree to a jagged peak and vanishes from sight.

CHARRED AND SMOKING WRECKAGE floats at the shore of the river. It is what remains of the firing platform
- the bodies of several of the Rainbow warriors still on board.
Smoke curls away from the platform and drifts through the forest. The only sound is the whinnying of a horse - it has a broken leg. Again and again it tries to get to its feet.
A solitary figure makes his way through the shadows. It's Will, soaking wet from the river. He stops at the entrance to the rocky gorge and looks at the carnage all around him. So much for knowledge and science. This is where the warriors of the tribes made their last stand - their bodies lie huddled together in a jumble.
Will stares at them, anguish on his face.

WILL
(softly, to himself)
I was so sure...
He kneels and turns one of the bodies over. It's Kip - speared through the chest. A shaft
of sunlight hits the Crescent of Light. It glints on his lifeless throat. Gently, he closes
Kip's glassy eyes. sound behind him. Will hurls himself aside, grabbing for a weapon.
He looks up -it's the Lookout, battle-stained and weary. Their eyes meet -

LOOKOUT
(quietly)
You said we'd win.
Will just nods - he knows.

LOOKOUT (CONT'D)
You gave us hope - that was the cruelest thing.
The Lookout kneels and crosses Kip's hands across his chest. He reaches down and
removes the Crescent of Light. He turns to Will -

LOOKOUT (CONT'D)
Get the weapons you need. The apes'll be coming back for their dead. Hurry!
Will arms himself with crossbows and arrows from the bodies.

CLOUDS OF SMOKE rise into the sky - the eagle's nest is on fire. Drak and his apes
make their way along a narrow mountain trail - they've put the humans' camp to the
torch.
With them is a long line of prisonerswomen and children mostly, many of them in tears.
They carry long poles over which are slung their dead and dying. We crane, up to -

HUGE ROCK OVERHANG high up the mountain-side. Standing underneath it,
hidden in shadow, are
Diamond and Strider. They look down on the mountain trail. Diamond sees
Eve.

THE MOUNTAIN TRAIL
The young girl stumbles along the road, tied by a length of chain to Drak's saddle. She's
bruised and bleeding, her ankles shackled, barely able to walk.

THE ROCK OVERHANG
Diamond looks at her, close to tears, but there's nothing she can do. She watches the
convoy wind along the trail.
Boomi The fire must have hit a store of gunpowder - an explosion rips through the
eagle's nest, blowing out the side of one of the peaks. Diamond watches the dust climb
into the sky. All her hopes seem to be going with it.

IN THE RIVER

It's twilight. Will and the Lookout are wading around a knob of land that protects one end of a tiny beach.
Will sees a fire burning on the sand, a cave opening off the beach, piles of stones like burial mounds.

WILL
What is this place?

LOOKOUT
It's called the Crossroads of the Fallen King - it's where our forefathers are laid to rest.
It's sacred to us - anyone who's still alive will make their way here.
They wade closer to the beach. In the firelight they see groups of tribesmen -survivors of the battle. Women and children - the lucky few who managed to flee the eagle's nest - are binding the warriors' wounds.
They look up - everyone falls silent at the sight of Will. As he comes closer he recognizes a woman, sitting alone -

WILL
It's Kip's wife. She's come from

THE EAGLE'S NEST -
He goes towards her, passing the other tribes-people. Nobody greets him.
They just watch him pass. He stops in front of Kip's wife. Her eyes are red from crying.

WILL rm sorry about your mate.
She says nothing - she just stares at him. Will keeps going -

WILL (CONT'D)
I've been to the eagle's nest. I was looking for the woman I was with. We searched but...
(he pauses)
What happened - was she captured?

KIP'S WIFE
I threw myself off a platform. I don't know what happened to anyone.
Will nods. He gets to his feet and moves to the women near the fire. We don't hear what he says, but we know what he is asking. One after another they shake their heads - no, they know nothing of Diamond.

SHAFT OF MOONLIGHT shimmers on the water. Will sits on a rock that straggles into the water.
His face is grim, his heart heavy with grief. He's making something with his hands - twisting and turning them - but in the dim light we can't see what it is.

INSIDE THE CAVE

A shaft of moonlight falls on a semi-circle of rock slabs standing on their end - it's like Stonehenge. The surviving tribes-people are gathered in their shadow.

OLD MAN
It's half a day since the battle. Any that survived would be here by now - we are all that remains of the Seven Tribes. The Ranger himself died on the field. We must decide ourselves what to do.
Silence for a moment. They have spent too long following a leader for discussion to come easily. Finally, a wounded warrior speaks -

WOUNDED WARRIOR
Like you say, Kip is dead. Maybe it's a sign -the Rangers have left Middle
Earth forever. Perhaps it's telling us to do the same.
A young woman - probably in her 20s - shakes her head.

YOUNG WOMAN
Leave the valley? This is where the eagles fly. This is their home. Nobody can live without their totem - we all know that!

LOOKOUT
Nobody can live with the apes eitherl If we stay here, we die. But if we travel beyond the Tower of the Moon, we've got a chance. Who knows - maybe our totems will follow us?
There's a murmur of agreement. It grows louder, tribes-people nodding their heads.

THE BEACH
Now we see what Will has been making - it's a boat made out of twigs and leaves. A tiny hull and a gaff-rigged mast. He leans forward and drops it in the water. He watches the current carry it away. Farther and farther it bobs out into the river -

WILL
(softly)
I'm sorry, Billie. I should have listened - it wasn't our war. All you wanted was a baby...
He can't go on. He watches the tiny boat disappear around the knob of land.

IN THE RIVER
The current carries the boat past a jagged boulder. An ape's hand reaches out and picks it up. He lifts it up to look more closely. We see his face - it's Strider. He turns the toy over in his hand, looking at it quizzically.
He hands it to Diamond, wading along behind him -

STRIDER
It looks like someone made it.

DIAMOND
It's a boat - it's gaff-rigged.

(realizing)
Oh, Jesus...
She plunges forward, wading as fast as she can.

DIAMOND (CONT'D)
Will!

ON THE BEACH
Will is walking up the beach. He stops, listening. He hears it again -his name! He turns and heads towards the river. He sees Diamond coming round the headland, splashing through the water.
Will stops. They look at one another - then they both move forward, arms stretching out. They wrap their arms around each other.

WILL
(softly)
I thought I'd lost you.

DIAMOND
I thought you were dead.
They keep holding each other.

WILL
How did you find this place?

DIAMOND
Strider. His father was a tracker. We've been following a trail for hours.
Will looks over her shoulder - Strider is wading towards them.

DIAMOND (CONT'D)
He saved my life, Will.
Will goes to greet him. The man and the ape embrace.

WILL
Thank you, my friend - thank you.

STRIDER
What did you expect? You would have done the same for me.

SHOWER OF SPARKS as Will puts a log on the fire. From inside the cave we hear the murmur of voices as the argument goes back and forth.
Both Diamond and Strider are wrapped in furs - their clothes are laid out next to the fire, drying. Will speaks to Diamond -

WILL

Some times when we want something so bad, we can take a thing and twist it in our head. You're sure about this, Billie?

DIAMOND
I'm pregnant, Will - I'm not crazy. She's not like them - she's a mutation.
Evolution's always trying to improve on itself. It's turned out a child that can walk taller and run faster, one whose brain-pan holds a mind that can think laterally. I've seen her, Will. I've held her in my arms - she was us.
Will looks at her. There's no doubt - he believes her.

WILL
You said she was with Drak.

DIAMOND
On a chain.

WILL
It's two days' march to the city. Was she wounded - can she make it?

DIAMOND
She can make it.
(a beat - she looks at him)
Will?
Before he can answer, the Old Man and several others come down the beach -

OLD MAN
It's decided - we're leaving the valley forever.
(turns to Strider)
Your people have won - the Seven Tribes of Middle Earth have been broken.
Long may their spirits haunt you
(he turns back to Will)
You and your mate can travel with u but we've got misery enough to carry.
Our hearth is not home to ny ape.

WILL
Then it's not home to us. The ape's better than any man I've known.
The Old Man's lip curls in a sneer. He shrugs and walks away.

STRIDER
Go with them. Will - everyone needs their own kind.
Will and Diamond newer almost simultaneously -

WILL
No!

DIAMOND

Of course we can't...
(to Will)
The city, Will.
Will and Strider turn nd look at her - incredulous.

WILL
We call it a city - it's more like a fortress, Billie. It can't be done.

DIAMOND
The three of you got out - everyone thought that was impossible too.

WILL
We were lucky. But that's the trouble with luck - it runs out. I don't want to be back in the city when it does.

DIAMOND
What about Eve - what do we do, just forget about her?

WILL
No. Maybe we can't stop the apes giving her the disease - but they'll have to turn her loose. That's the only way she can infect others. So we lay a plan and we find her. Then it's our job to stop her having children. If we can do that, it can't be passed on through the race.
She shrugs That's the only thing I can think of.

DIAMOND
How long will that take - less than twenty-five days ?

WILL
No.
DIAMOND So what of my child?
We have to face it - you're going to lose it.
She turns away, trying to keep her emotions in check. Will comes to her side -

WILL (CONT'D)
We can't take our eye off the goal. If we solve this, you can have other children. Not if wa throw our lives away, though.

DIAMOND
Whose, Will - whose children?
She looks at him. He meets her gaze. A beat.

WILL guess that's your call.

DIAMOND

What sort of father would you make? You told me once the only thing that matters is knowledge. That's wrong. Science and technology can only take you so far - in the end it's our humanity that maners. That's what makes us great. You're a wonderful scientist, Will -but what sort of person are you?
What would you do if it was your child?
She looks straight into his eyes. Finally he answers. Softly -

WILL
I don't know how to do it - not the humanity part, that's easy compared to getting into the city. I just don't know...
He picks up a stick and starts to scratch out a rough map on the ground.

WILL (CONT'D)
It sits on a river. There's only one bridge -heavily guarded. Even if we could cross it, all the ridges and roads are patrolled -

STRIDER
There's one place that's not.
Both Diamond and Will turn to him. He takes the stick -

STRIDER (CONT'D)
Down here - it's called Funeral Rock. It sits at the bottom of the temple.
From there you can make your way into the city. Even so, you still have to cross the river.
He draws an arrow across the water, illustrating the problem. Diamond is about to speak but she looks at Will - he's staring at the arrow, an idea, half formed, is starting to form.

WILL
Maybe there is a way...across the river, I mean.

DIAMOND
How?
Will turns to her -

WILL
You'll love it - there's barely any science to it at all.

DIAMOND
We're going? Is that right - we're going!?
Their eyes meet and hold. He smiles at her.

THREE SILHOUETTES travel fast along a high ridge. The sun - a fiery disc - rises right behind them. We recognize their physiques - Will in the lead, then Diamond and Strider. As they cross the face of the sun, we dissolve to -

LIGHTS TWINKLE on the buildings and terraces of the apes' city. Will and his two comrades are on a bluff, looking down. The sound of music and laughter drifts towards them on the night air. Suddenly a huge tongue of flame shoots out of a stone chimney.

STRIDER
They've started up the furnace.
(softly)
Let the games begin.

DIAMOND
What games?

WILL
The apes kill their prisoners for sport. The furnace takes care of the bodies.
Diamond - sickened by it - turns to look at Will. Already he's heading off, leading them down nrrow trail.

A HIDDEN LEDGE much closer to the city. Will and the others move fast along it, deep in the shadows. The river thunders by below them, separating them from the city. The only way across is the massive iron and wood bridge. Ape guards patrol it.
Only Diamond pauses to look et it. Will and Strider urge her forward. It disappears from view.

A STEEL ARROW flies through the air. Tied to its shaft, trailing out behind, is a rope made from vines. Will lowers a crossbow. He watches the arrow fly through the mist and spray -

THE RIVER races by just below and pours over the Falls of No Return. Whack! The arrow buries itself in the trunk of a massive tree standing on the bank.

ON THE OTHER SHORE
Will and Strider haul the rope taut and tie it round a tree. It stretches from one side of the river to the other. All it has to do is hold. Will turns to Diamond. He shouts to be heard over the roar of the falls -

WILL
You first. We'll be right behind.
Diamond scrambles up on to a rock platform and grabs hold of the rope. She looks across the riverthe moonlight spills through the wind-blown spray; the roaring water rushes by; the rope hangs like a thread. There's fear on her face -

WILL (CONT'D)
You ready?

DIAMOND
It sure as shit ain't Kansas, is it?

WILL
Go!
Diamond throws herself forward. Her feet leave the platform. Hand over hand she goes
- out across the river.
Will watchel for a moment then launches himself - his hands wrap around the rope.
Strider slings his crossbow over his shoulder and jumps. The line bows under his
weight. Diamond'l feet drop closer to the water. She looks down - the mass of black
water, flecked with foam, rushes past.
Will looks ahead - Diamond is almost lost in flurries of spray. She's dripping wet,
hauling herself forward -
The sound of the Falls is deafening. Right below her, a huge, swirling
"hole" opens up. It's a whirlpool. She starts to swing across it. Joltl

THE TREE TRUNK
The arrow pulls part way out of the tree. The steel shaft shivers but it holds. Everything
seems okay. Suddenly -
Snap! One of the strands of the vine breaks -

ON THE ROPE
Everything bucks and shudders. Diamond screams. She looks down - straight into the
vortex of the whirlpool. Her blood runs cold - she freezes.

**WILL SEES HER HANGING MOTIONLESS ON THE ROPE. HE SCREAMS
AT HER -**
WILL
Go! Billie - go!
She doesn't seem to hear. Her eyes are wide with fear - staring down, down into the
whirlpool's bottomless well.

**WILL, TRYING TO GET TO HER, HURLS HIMSELF FORWARD. THE
ROPE STRAINS AND
BOWS -**
WILL
Move!
She doesn't react. Strider watches as Will tries to catch up. The rope is swaying so much
it's agonizingly slow.
Diamond stares at a huge log spinning down into nothingness. The whirlpool seems to
be swallowing everything, even the moonlight -

WILL (CONT'D)
Billiai What about the baby?!
The word hits her. She pulls her eyes from the swirling death. She looks at
Will.

WILL (CONT'D)

Move, Billiel Nowl

She understands. She starts to pull herself forward. Will slumps with relief -

ON THE SHORE

The arrow moves another inch out of the trunk. The rope fixed to its shaft is strained to breaking point. But still everything holds...

THE IRON AND WOOD BRIDGE

One of the guards patrols the bridge. Out of the corner of his eye - flash of something. He looks towards the Falls.

GUARD

(calling)

Gimla.

The other guard joins him. They peer through the night at the spray rising from the Falls. They see it again - above the river, a flash of light on metal.

The keep watching. An eddy of wind clears the mist for a second. They see

Strider going hand over hand along the rope, moonlight glinting on his crossbow.

ON THE SHORE

Another strand of the rope breaks. We follow it as it unravels - past

Diamond and Will. Before we get to Strider it stops - a section of the rope is so badly frayed it can't go any farther. It's going to break any moment.

Screech! A siren wails.

STRIDER

They've seen usl Will looks up-river to the bridge. Through a hole in the mist he sees ape guards pointing and yelling. A whole squadron runs to join them.

Diamond throws herself forward - she makes the shorel

Will and Strider give it everything they've got. Strider's first hand passes the frayed section. He's following it with his second -

Snap! The whole rope breaks. Will - closest to the shore - plunges into the ripping current. But at lealt he's clinging to the rope with both hands.

Strider's in the water hanging on to the end of the rope by the fingers of one paw. Will turns and reaches for him.

STRIDER (CONT'D)

No! Save yourselfl

ON THE SHORE

Diamond has grabbed hold of the rope and is trying to pull it in. The weight - of the men and the current - make it impossible. All she can do is try and hold them.

ON THE ROPE

Strider's fingers are slipping free. Will grabs him - man and ape, hand to paw. Will holds him.

STRIDER
We'll both die. Let go! Will shakes his head - no. Hanging on to the rope one-handed,
the current tearing at his body, he tries to haul Strider in.
Whizz! An arrow flies past, just missing them, and plunges into the water.
The apes on the bridge are firing.

STRIDER (CONT'D)
Another minute, we'll both be dead. Do it, Will!
Will tries again to drag Strider to the rope. Another arrow flies through the mist and
spray - even closer. Strider reaches out with his free hand.
He starts to prize Will's fingers loose -

STRIDER (CONT'D)
If nothing else, I made it to the Falls No Return.
Will realizes - nothing is going to stop Strider.

WILL
The sacred words, Strider - what are the words?!

STRIDER
"In the beginning...

WILL
'In the beginning was the word and the word wes God...'

STRIDER
(in wonder)
You know the words?

WILL
You'll walk in the next world, Strider.

STRIDER
How do you know?

WILL
I've seen the future, haven't I?
Strider smiles at him - a smile of perfect peace.

STRIDER
Good-bye Will. Take care of Billie.
He twists Will's last finger free. He drops - the swirling river carries him away. Will is
close to tears, but he won't let himself cry. Two more arrows sizzle past -

WILL

And the word was God. Yea, though I walk through the valley of death, I will fear no evil...
Strider spins down the river, through the spray and foam.

WILL (O.S.) (CONT'D)
Surely goodness and mercy shall follow me all the days of my life and I will dwell in the house of the Lord forever. Amen.
Strider, one arm raised, plunges over the Falls.

ON THE BRIDGE
We see who's been coordinating the firing. It's Drak. Archers are kneeling on the bridge, trying to sight a target through the foaming water and clouds of mist.
Drak, never taking his eyes off of the river, draws back the massive spring of his crossbow and reloads.

ON THE SHORE
Diamond ia hauling on the rope, pulling it in. Will, up to his neck in water, tows himself along it. His feet find a footing - he starts to scramble up the bank. Diamond goes towards him -
Just for a moment, the mist clears.

ON THE BRIDGE moment's long enough. Drak's seen him. In one fluid movement he adjusts his aim and fires -

ON THE SHORE
Diamond is almost in Will's arms. Sswhack! The arrow rips into WiU's back, through his ribs. He pitches forward. Diamond screams. He falls into her arms.
The mist closes around them.

HUGE STONE ARCH
The survivors of the Seven Tribes travel fast along a forest trail. All of them are burdened down with possessions, weary from the road - they are leaving the valley.
Kip's Wife and the Old Man are in the lead. They pass through the arch, out into a clearing. In the middle of it is a fire, shadows camped around it -
Kip's wife and the other survivors stop in fear. One of the shadows rises from the. fire. Bathed in moonlight - almost ghost-like - he comes towards them. It's Aragorn!
Kip's wife moves forward and embraces him -

KIP'S WIFE
We thought you were dead.

ARAGORN
Hunted, but not dead. A dozen of us were driven back in the battle -
He indicates his men. They are coming forward, greeting the survivors. The Young Woman sees her mate - she cries out. They hold each other.

ARAGORN (CONT'D)
For three days a squadron of apes have tracked us. Last night we ambushed them. We're heading now for the eagle's nest.

KIP'S WIFE
(softly)
There is no eagle's nest.
Aragorn stares at her, not wanting to believe it.

KIP'S WIFE (CONT'D)
We're all that's left of the Seven Tribes.
Grief wells up inside Aragorn. We hold on his face.

A FIRE CRACKLES
All of the tribes-people are gathered around it.

OLD MAN
There is no-one else, Aragorn - you are the Ranger.

ARAGORN
(shaking his head)
No. We must all follow the trail we think best. You've decided yours. For me * I'll go to the city of the apes and take what revenge I can. I'll go alone - but like the traveler, I think death will be the only thing I find there.

OLD MAN
Then it will find us, too. Warriors follow their Ranger. That's always been the way of it in Middle Earth.

ARAGORN
But nothing's the same now. Think of the women-folk. What will become of them?

KIP'S WIFE
You're right - there's so few of us now, nothing is the same. You must allow the women to follow, too.
ARAGORN But women can't fight.
KIP'S WIFE Women have never been allowed to fight. That doesn't mean they can't.
All the women nod their assent. The men smile, agreeing. Everyone waits for Aragorn to decide. A beat - then he nods his head and smiles.
The tribes-people start to cheer. The Lookout steps forward. From out of the folds of his fur, he takes the Crescent of Light. All of the tribe stare at it.

LOOKOUT
I found it on the battlefield. There were those who said the Rangers had left Middle Earth forever - I didn't know what to do with it.

He hands it to Aragorn. The whole tribe watches as the proud man once again ties the talisman of his rank around his neck.

ARAGORN
Douse the fire. The Seven Tribes are going to war.

ON THE SHORE
The apes, carrying torches, search the river bank and surrounding cliffs.
We push in on a pool of darkness behind them -
Will and Diamond hide in a hollow beneath the tangled roots of a huge tree.
They have done their best to dress Will's wound but he's obviously in a lot of pain -

DIAMOND
You can't go on, Will - not like this.

WILL
What about the baby?

DIAMOND
I'll keep going - I'll try and get Eve.

WILL
Alone? Don't be ridiculous -
He starts to haul himself to his feet. His face twists in pain - he has to stop.

DIAMOND
Look at you - you can barely walk.
He puts out his hand, needing I boost up.

WILL
If I can just get up - help me.
Diamond shakes her head - no. They look at one another.

WILL (CONT'D)
Don't do this to me - pleasel

DIAMOND
You've done enough - more than anyone else could. You're one of the finest men
I've ever known - but it's over, Will. You're going to have to wait. Now it's my turn -
She grabs her weapons and starts to leave. Will makes it to his feet -

WILL
Billie!She's almost through the tangled roots.

WILL (CONT'D)

I made a mistake once - I went on a journey with someone I loved. At the end, I let her
go into danger alone.
Diamond stops.

DIAMOND
Where was that - Berkeley, Will?
She turns and looks at him. He nods his head - yes.

DIAMOND (CONT'D)
What happened?

WILL
I knew I'd found the chemical key. I was working with three young researchers. One of
them was a woman called Ali Conoily. We were engaged.
They were the ones that went into the tanks. I didn't know as much as I thought I did.
They died in there.

DIAMOND
Why didn't you go, Will?

WILL
We all wanted to. It was a great adventure. Wa drew lots for it. I should never have
agreed, but we were young - and like the young we thought life would last forever.

DIAMOND
Robert Plant died too, didn't he - in a way?

WILL
The experiment was unauthorized. There was an inquiry. They said the theory had no
basis. 'Ludicrous" was a word they used. My career had gone up like a rocket. It came
down like the stick. I couldn't find work anywhere

DIAMOND
"Will Robinson" - that was your joke, I guess. You were Lost in Space, were you?

WILL
Yeah, but I never realized it'd be so appropriate.
They sort of smile at one another.

WILL (CONT'D) had twenty years to work out where my research went wrong - so
what, though. It was just a mind game. But I've learnt a lot of things - the most important
is that sometimes you get a second chance. A second chance for a lot of things -
He looks straight at her. They hold each other's eyes.

WILL (CONT'D)
And when you do, you have to grab it and make sure you never let it go.

I've got the heart, Billie. It's my body that's failing me.
Neither one of them moves. A beat.

DIAMOND
Give me your hand, Will.
She helps him to his feet.

A GIANT CHASM
It's several hours before dawn. In the gloom - whooshl Kip's Wife rides a flying fox across a precipitous drop.
She lands on the other side of a jagged ravine. The rest of the tribe, all heavily armed, are waiting there. They turn end run, fading into the trees.

THE FUNERAL ROCK juts out into the roaring river. Will and Diamond scramble out of the darkness and land on the rock. Will's face is haggard with pain but he forces himself forward. He's loosening up. going faster as he moves -
They pass through the huge legs of the stone ape - into the Temple.

A DARKENED ROOM
Torches flicker on the walls. From somewhere close-by - muffled - we hear the sound of a crowd. A young ape, barely in his teens, stands in the middle of the room, almost naked. His face is painted with strange ochre markings.
A circle of ape warriors watch as Ma-Gog lifts a slender blade. Intoning words in some strange tongue, he slices the blade across the Teenager's forehead. The Teenager winces but he doesn't cry out - this is his manhood ceremony.

THE STABLES
The sound of the crowd is much louder here but still we don't see them. The prisoners from the Eagle's Nest are crowded into the corrals.
One of the gates is thrown open. Three ape guards enter. They push the tribes-people aside and grab a 12-year old boy. His mother clings to him, screaming. One of the guards drags her off and they haul the boy out of the corral.

AN ARENA
-like a small bullring - in the center of the stables. Now we see the crowd
- apes, all males, sit in the bleachers. They roar as a door is opened and the young Tribe-Boy is pushed into the ring.
He looks around the arena - yelling, screaming apes. Terror on his face. An even louder roar goes up. The Boy turns -
The Teenage ape steps out of a tunnel, the ochre markings on his face like war-paint, the blood barely dried on his forehead. He carries spears and a club.
One of the apes throws a couple of captured human weapons down to the Boy.
The Teenage ape moves in on him. He is a warrior now - this is going to be his first kill.

IN THE CORRAL

The Boy's mother is huddled down, being comforted by other tribes-people. A huge roar goes up from the arena as the first blow is struck. The sound carries over to -

A TERRACE

Drak is alone, walking a high ridge. He stops, looking down on the twinkling lights. The city is virtually deserted but Drak doesn't move - he's uneasy, troubled by something he can't put a name to.

THE COOL AND LOVELY ROOM

The five baby apes sit on cots. They watch as Doctor Zora inserts a syringe into the smallest ape's arm. The baby starts to cry. Doctor Zora comforts her as she draws out a cup of blood. She turns to her assistant, Ben-Guri

DOCTOR ZORA

Is the girl animal ready?

BEN-GURI

They're doing it now.

INSIDE THE LABORATORY

Eve is struggling and crying as an ape guard carries her towards an operating table. He and another guard start to strap her down.

The Vet works at the bench, heating a steel needle over a flame. It's the same sort of catheter that was used on Will - one end of the needle attached to a long tube. A knock on the door.

VET

That must be Zors with the blood.

One of the guards goes and unbolts the door. He recoils - it's Will.

Sswhack! He fires the first bolt from a double-barreled crossbow. It takes the guard in the chest.

He and Diamond dive into the room. Eve starts hollering. The second guard is wheeling, crossbow rising. He rifle-butts Diamond across the head. Her weapon goes flying.

The guard is aiming. Will is on the floor, tumbling. Barely time to aim, on his back, firing overhead, he shoots -

Whack! Bullseye. The arrow hits the guard dead in the heed.

The Vet grabs the first guard's fallen crossbow. He aims at Will. Diamond screams a warning but there's nothing Will can do - he's struggling to reload, one-handed because of his wounds.

Diamond - unarmed - scoops the red-hot syringe off the bench. The Vet reaches for the trigger. Diamond leaps forward. She drives the syringe into his chest.

The Vet stands goggle-eyed. Diamond must have found his heart - a torrent of blood pours down the clear tube. It spills on to the floor. The Vet topples forward.

Slash! Slash! Will cuts throughthe straps that tie Eve to the table.

OUTSIDE THE HALL OF LEARNING

Drak turns a corner of the building. He stops and touches the ground with his finger. He lifts it to his mouth and tastes it. He rises to his feet, following trail of blood.

A TORCH is ripped from a bracket. It's Drak.. He shines it down into a stone well. The flame splits the darkness. Floating in the water at the bottom of the well is an ape guard -dead, an arrow through his throat.

IN THE ARENA
The Tribe-Boy is sprawled in the dust, bleeding badly from a rip across his ribs. His spear lies next to him, a wooden shield raised across his head.
The Teenage ape , rains blows down on it with a sword.
The apes in the bleachers are cheering wildly. Smash! The shield splinters.
The sword slices the Boy's arm -

APES
Kill! Kill! Kill!
The Boy stares up - the Teenage smiles and raises his sword.
Shriek! The alarm sounds. Everything freezes. Then officers are on their feet, yelling orders. Ape soldiers grab their weapons, heading for the doors.
The Teenage ape looks around, robbed of his moment. The Boy sees his chance. He raises his spear and drives it deep into the ape's groin. He staggers and falls - on top of the Boy.
The apes pour out of the arena. The siren carries over to -

A STONE CORRIDOR
Will's got Eve slung over his shoulder. They're stumbling down a corridor - past other labs and research rooms. They burst through a sat of doors, into

-

A COURTYARD at the back of the Hall of Learning. It's deep in shadow. From behind they hear the sound of pounding feet. Will looks around, not sure which way to go. He glances across a terrace - the doors to the stables fly open. The ape warriors charge out.

WILL
Can you ride?
Diamond nods her head - yes. He thrusts Eve into her hands -

WILL (CONT'D)
Go for the stables. Head for the eagle's nest. I'll try to join you there.
Diamond hesitates - she doesn't want to leave him.

DIAMOND
What are you going to do?

WILL
Delay them. Now go, Billie. Go!

THE PRIMITIVE ELEVATOR rops down the side of the ravine. Standing on it are Nazgul and about

THE PRIMITIVE ELEVATOR a dozen Praetorian Guards. Nazgul looks down - torches and fires in drums are lighting up the streets and terraces. Ape soldiers are running everywhere - searching.

ON THE GROUND
The flame-thrower rolls along a street. The driver's canopy is hidden by flapping tarpaulins. In the chaos nobody pays it any attention.

ON THE ELEVATOR
Nazgul sees the machine rolling towards them.

NAZGUL
That's strange - why does Drak need the Flame?
Suddenly he realizel. He turns, screaming up at the apes controlling the mechanism.

NAZGUL (CONT'D)
Stopl Take it backl

THE FLAME-THROWER dead guard is draped over the side of the machine, blood dripping from his headWill is in the cabin, working the controls. He sees the elevator slow in mid-descent. He throws a lever forward. For a moment, nothing. Then -
Whoosh! A huge tongue of flame blasts out of the barrel.
Two of the guards are trying to climb the ropes. Nazgul is wheeling around in a panic.
The flame hits them! The whole wooden structure catches fire.
We see the apes through the flames, struggling and writhing.
The ropes burn through. The blazing structure plummets down -

THE CENTRAL SQUARE
Smash! It hits the ground in a shower of blazing timbers and dead apes. Ape soldiers - standing nearby - stare in shock. The smell of roasted ape fills the air.

EVE SITS ALONE
She's on the floor of the stables, deep in shadow. She's scared, looking ahead -
The first weak light of dawn shines through the open doors. We see an ape guard, keys jangling from his waist, on petrol.
He hears something - a rock falling, a rustle of movement. Raising his weapon, he moves towards a pool of black shadow, past a pile of rocks, into an alcove.
Diamond rises out of the rocks behind him. He spins - she's got her cross-bow raised. Point-blank range. She nails him.

THE PRISONERS are shackled in the corrals. They see Diamond running out of the shadows towards them. She tossel them the keys -

DIAMOND
Arm yourselves. Find Will - he needs youl She turns and goes. The prisoners start to
unlock the chains.

EVE smiles as Diamond races out of the shadows, sweeps her up and keeps running.

IN THE ARENA
The Teenage ape and the Boy lie where they fell, their spilt blood staining the dust.
The Boy's mother scrambles over the deserted bleachers and goes to her son.
She drags off the ape. Her son's eyes are closed, his arms lacerated, his chest wounded
and crusted with blood. She stares at him - he doesn't move.
She starts to sob. The Boy's eyes flicker open. They look at one another.
The motheY gathers him into her arms. He's alive! He's alive!
The sound of a horse. The mother turns, fearful. She looks across the arena, through a
railing -

IN THE CORRALS
Diamond gallops a stallion through the corrals. Eve's clutching the saddle in front of
her - hair flying, her eyes sparkling with exhilaration. The stallion gallops faster.
The prisoners - unchaining the last of their comrades - turn and look. It's a magnificent
sight. Diamond is crouched Iow over the flying horse.
Straight ahead - a railed fence, part of the corral.
She leaps the horse over it. They land. In front - another hurdle. Again she does it.
The prisoners stare. Diamond charges towards the open doors of the stables.

CLOUDS OF SMOKE AND FLAME
The crashed elevator hal set the surrounding buildings on fire. Ape city is burning.
The Flame stands on a steep incline, its back wedged against the wall of a terrace.
Whooshl Fire shoots out of its barrel as Will keeps a horde of ape soldiers at bay.
The soldiers turn - Drak, surrounded by the Praetorian Guard, gallops straight towards
them. He'l not stopping for anything - the soldiers scramble aside.

IN THE CABIN
Will sees Drak and the guards appear through the swirling clouds of smoke.
They look like the horsemen of the apocalypse. As Will throws the lever we sea a
primitive gauge above his head. It's in the red -

IN THE SQUARE
Whoosh! The tongue of flame shoots through the smoke. It touches the guards with a
deadly kiss, throwing them screaming from their horses. But Drak blasts through -

IN THE CABIN
Will is engulfed in a backdraft of black oily smoke. He peers through it -
Drak charges towards him! Will hits the lever again. The flame erupts from the barrel.
Then it dies - out of fuel.

WILL
Shit!

IN THE SQUARE
Drak gallops forward. He raises weapon - a shoulder-mounted harpoon. He aims -

IN THE CABIN
Will throws himself aside. He smashes both hands down on a lever on the floor. A hiss of steam. The machine lurches forward -

IN THE SQUARE
Drak tries to get a clear shot at Will. The machine gathers speed down the incline, coming straight towards Drak. He veers his horse aside and wheels around. He charges alongside the cabin - it's empty

ON THE MACHINE
Will clings to the outside of the Flame as it roars across the smoke-filled square. He's out of sight of Drak - but not for long. The ape and his stallion loom into view behind the machine, Will scrambles back into the cabin -

IN THE SQUARE
Apes are scattering as the runaway machine flies across the square. Drak is at full gallop, veering from one side of the Flame to the other. Will clambers back and forth - cat and mouse at full tilt.
Drak swings his horse close to the back of the machine. He stands up in the stirrups, the harpoon clamped to his shoulder - he's going on board!
The Flame flies out of the square and down a street. An ape throws himself into a doorway - just in time, Drak steadies himself, about to jump.
Suddenly his horse whinnies wildly. Drak looks ahead - holy shit!. They're heading straight for the front of a blazing house.
Drak throws himself down into the saddle and hauls on the reins. Will hurls himself back into the cabin, arms shielding his head. Smash! The Flame crashes through the front wall -

INSIDE THE HOUSE
The barrel of the Flame acts like a battering ram - it blasts through the walls in a shower of burning timbers. It crashes through the kitchen and stops in a courtyard.
Will clambers out of the cabin and drops to the ground. A yell goes up - apes are coming through the adjoining houses. Will turns and heads down an alleyway.

CITY STREET
Diamond's horse flies down a street - a high terrace towers on one side, a row of burning buildings on the other. The road turns right. She swings around it - apes! A platoon of them right in front of her. She screams at
Eve -

DIAMOND
Hold on!
She throws herself aside, pulling on the reins. The horse spins in a
U-turn, grazing past a burning building. Diamond gallops back the way she came.
Crash! The wall of a burning building in front of her collapses. Blazing beams block
the road. The horse shies away. Diamond wheels him around -
The apes race into the road. She looks around desperately - she's trapped.
She grabs Eve and awingl her onto the saddle behind her - she'll be safer there.
She spurs the horse forward and crouches Iow in the saddle - she's going to charge
straight through the apes. They drop to one knee - the firing position - and raise their
weapons. A dozen crossbowl aim straight at
Diamond.
There's no way out - she flies towards them. Whizzl The sound of arrows.
But it's not the apes - they go down like nine-pins.
Diamond looks up - Aragorn has arrived! Backlit by the rising sun, the men and women
of the Tribes are pouring volley after volley into the apes.
Nobody fires better than Kip's Wife.
Diamond leaps the horse through the dead and dying apes and turns down the road.

MA-GOG stands on a terrace, his cloak blowing in the wind, his one cruel eye blazing
with anger. Flanked by two ape warriors, he looks down on the burning buildings.
The freed prisoners are waging a pitched battle outside the stables.
Ma-Gog sees Will - he's running along the rooftops, leaping from one building to the
next. Ma-Gog points at him, yelling at apes in the streets below -

MA-GOG (CONT'D)
Kill him! In the name of God, kill himl Sswhish! The blade of a sword cleaves through
frame. It cuts one of the ape warriors from neck to waist.
Ma-Gog spins - it's Aragorn, armed to the teeth, behind them.
The second warrior goes for him. Aragorn has dropped the sword. He raises a crossbow
and fires. The bolt shatters the ape's armor and buries itself in his chest.
Ma-Gog swirls aside his cloak. In his good hand he holds a double-edged sword.
Aragorn drops the crossbow ands ducks beneath Ma-Gog's arcing blow.
He lunges with a short-handled spear -

ARAGORN
For my peoplc!
It takes Ma-Gog in the gut. His one eye bulges. Aragorn rips the spcar out

-

ARAGORN (CONT'D)
And this - for my daughterl He drives the spear into the High Priest's heart. The cruel
eye flickers and dies.

ON THE ROOFTOP

Will has seen it all. He screams -

WILL
Behind you! Aragorn - behind!

ON THE TERRACE
Aragorn turns. It's Drak, on horseback, thundering down on him. But the leader of the
Seven Tribes knows no fear - only the memory of his lost child.
He raises his second spear and charges straight at Drak. The huge ape levels the
shoulder-mounted harpoon. He pulls the trigger. Sswang! The powerful spring on the
barrel releases, the harpoon trails a length of rope behind it -
Wham! The harpoon smashes through Aragorn's chest. He dies as he falls.

ON THE ROOFTOP
Will stares in anguish. He turns away - he sees Diamond. She's at full gallop - Eve
clinging to her back - charging along a road several terraces below. She's got a clear run
for the iron bridge and freedom.
Will looks across at Drak - he's seen her too! For a moment the two of them stare at one
another. Will's face is drawn and haggard from the injuries he carries.
Drak's lip curls in a sneer - he knows he's going to win. He beats his chest with his fists
and spurs the stallion over the edge of the terrace, going for Diamond.
Will runs as fast as his body will let him - along the rooftop.

INSIDE A HOUSE
An ape mother cowers in a corner, her two children clutched to her, the sounds of battle
all around. She looks up in terror -
Smash! Will's feet blast through the roof. He lands on the floor, crossbow raised -but
not st her. Framed in the front doorway is an ape warrior on horseback. Wham! Will
shoots him and runs for the horse.

DIAMOND and Eve fly down charred street .They head towards a large open square.

OUTSIDE THE STABLES
Smoke and dust swirl through the air. The freed prisoners are fighting ape infantry. Drak
races past the battle. The rope from the harpoon is tied around the saddle, dragging
Aragorn's body through the dust.
He looks ahead - Diamond gallops across the square. Drak whips his horse forward -

A CURVED ROAD on a high terrace. Flying around a corner - Will! His coat is
billowing, the horse's mane streaming in the wind. He hits the straight-away and gallops
even faster.
He looks down on the road below - Diamond is ahead but Drak is gaining on her. Will
plunges into a tunnelhewn out of rock.

ON THE ROAD

Eve clings tight to Diamond's waist. The little girl looks back - Drak is thundering behind them, pennants snapping in the wind, armor glinting on the horse's chest. It's an awesome sight.

Drak has the reins in his teeth. He's using both hands to reload the harpoon.

Diamond sees the bridge dead ahead. Heavily armed apes have barricaded it.

She curses and yanks the bridle. The horse sweeps around an island in the center of the road - a huge monument to some dead ape. She gallops back the way she came, almost passing Drak. He charges round the island.

OUT OF THE TUNNEL comes Will. He looks down to the lower road - Diamond and Drak are coming back towards him! He turns the horse around - back into the tunnel. Whooshl He flies out the other end, into daylight. He looks over his shoulder - he's in front of them but thirty feet too high. He digs his heels into the horse's flanks -over a Iow wall they fly. God knows where it goes -

DOWN A ROCKY SUDE into a dead-end cul-de-sac just above the roadway. Apesi Two of them are guarding the Claw and the Bells. Will fires from the shoulder - he drops the first ape.

The second ape aims at him. Will raises another crossbow. They fire almost simultaneously. Will throws himself aside, out of the saddle. The horse rears and bolts. Will looks up from the dirt - the ape has Will's arrow embedded in his chest. He falls forward - dead.

Will scrambles to a parapet and looks down on the road just below. Diamond and Eve - clinging to the horse for dear life - race towards him. Will grabs a crossbow and struggles to reload. He can't - it takes the strength of both arms to cock it,

ON THE ROAD
Diamond's horse is lathered in sweat, almost blown. Eve looks over her shoulder, her eyes wide with fear - Drak is close behind, gaining at every step.

IN THE CUL-DE-SAC
Will leaps from the Balls on to the Claw.

ON THE ROAD
Drak swings the harpoon on to his shoulder. He sights down the barrel. Eve sees the weapon lock on to their backs. She screams a warning et Diamond -

EVE
Billie!
Diamond leaps the horse over a charred wagon abandoned on the road. Drak loses her in his sights. He follows her over the wagon.

ON THE CLAW
Will is in the driver's seat. He throws a lever - nothing happens. He tries another -the long jib that supportl the two iron jews swings towards the road.

DRAK aims the harpoon. He's got Eve end Diamond, one behind the other, in his sights.

DRAK
A bargain - two for the price of onel

ON THE CLAW
Will spins a small steering wheel.

ON THE ROAD
Drak is close behind Diamond. The harpoon's massive spring is coiled.
Drak's finger curls around the trigger, about to fire.
Suddenly he screams - dropping right in front, coming straight towards him, are the opening jaws of the Claw.

WILL JERKS BACK ANOTHER LEVER -
WILL
Keep your hands off her, you dirty ape.
The jaws lock clean around Drak's waist, plucking him off the saddle and lifting him up into the air. He's still got the harpoon. He sees Will at the control. He swings the barrel round -
Will hits a switch. Wrong one - nothing happens.
Drak's got him in his sights. His finger finds the trigger -
Will throws another switch.
The jaws start to close! Drak tries to pull the trigger - he can't, his body is twisting. The jaws are crushing him! He musters all of his strength and tries to fire. He and Will look straight at one another. A beat. Drsk's finger starts to slide off the trigger -

IN THE SQUARE
Apes stare up at their warrior lord, clamped in the Clew. He let out a blood curdling scream. The bottom half of his torso - everything from the waist down - falls towards the ground. Maybe it's just the wind, but the legs still seem to be kicking.
The apes reel beck in horror. With mighty battle cry, the tribes-people - the prisoners end Aregom'l followers - hurl themselves forward, attacking.
The apes break end start to run.

ON THE ROAD
Diamond end Eve have dismounted. Diamond stumbles forward - Will is coming towards her. She holds out her arms and they embrace. Neither one says a word, they just hold each other tight.

CLOUDS OF SMOKE almost obscure the setting sun. Will and Diamond stand on the iron bridge watching the tribes-people. They've harnessed horses to ropes tied around the statues on the avenue of idols - one after another the stone monoliths come crashing down.

DIAMOND

If nothing else, we helped the tribes take back their valley.

WILL
Our valley, too Billia.
She looks at him - questioning.

WILL (CONT'D)
There's one thing I never told you - I never worked out how to get back.
She smiles at him.

DIAMOND
A small point. But give me some credit. I'm a scientist - I knew that.

WILL
(in wonder)
But you came anyway.

DIAMOND
That was love.

WILL
For the baby?
She shakes her head.

DIAMOND
For the both of you.
They stare into each other's eyes. They kiss.

DIAMOND (CONT'D)
I only have one regret. We'll never know if we succeeded.

WILL
Of course we will. You're pregnant - if the baby's born alive, we'll know it worked.

SUNLIGHT GLISTENS ON THE OCEAN
The surf rolls in on a golden beach. At the water's edge, a line of footprints. We follow them to find Will on top of a rocky cliff. He's building something out of iron and rock and sand but we can't make out what it is.

DIAMOND (O.S.)
Will
He turns and runs to the mouth of a large cave.

INSIDE THE CAVE
Diamond lies on her back on a pile of animal skins. Her belly is exposed, heavy with the unborn child. Eve crouches next to her, trying to help.

WILL
It's started?
She nods her head then grimaces with pain as another contraction starts.

THE SUN IS SETTING ON THE SEA
From inside the cave, we hear Diamond scream.

IN THE CAVE
Will kneels between Diamond's legs. Her face, glistening with sweat; is a mask of pain.
She holdl Eve's hind tight and pushes.
Will, half hidden by her upraised legs, delivers the child. Diamond raises herself up -
trying to See her child. Neither she nor us can see it's face.
We push in on Will. Ha raises his hand and slaps the baby's rump. No sound.
Ha raises his hand again - suddenly the baby starts to cry. Now we see the baby - a
perfect little boy.
Eve laughs. Diamond smiles. Tears fill her eyes. She and Will look at one another. He
comes towards her and tenderly places the baby in her arms.

THE CAVE
Will and Eve help Diamond. She comes out of the cave, still holding the baby. It's magic
hour - they stand on a rock ledge, looking at the ocean washed with color from the
setting sun.
We see what Will was building. It's sort of like a sculpture - just the head and crown of
the Statue of Liberty.
Diamond smiles. She looks at him, wondering why -

WILL
It's to make sure we never forget where we came from.
The baby starts to cry. Will puts one arm each around Diamond and Eve.
We pull back from them - high up into the stars. The baby's cry carries over. We see
earth rise. In all this nothingness - life. back

www.ingramcontent.com/pod-product-compliance
Lightning Source LLC
Chambersburg PA
CBHW080911160726
48000CB00009B/2946